WriteTraits®

TEACHER'S GUIDE

Vicki Spandel

Grade 4

GReaT SOuRCe®

EDUCATION GROUP

A Houghton Mifflin Company

Vicki Spandel

Vicki Spandel was codirector of the original teacher team that developed the six-trait model and has designed instructional materials for all grade levels. She has written several books, including *Creating Writers—Linking Writing Assessment and Instruction* (Longman), and is a former language arts teacher, journalist, technical writer, consultant, and scoring director for dozens of state, county, and district writing assessments.

Cover: Illustration by Claude Martinot Design.

Design: The Mazer Corporation

Printed in the United States of America

International Standard Book Number: 0-669-49043-1

8 9 10 - BA - 06

Contents

Introduction

Unit 1: Ideas

Unit 5: Sentence Fluency

Unit 6: Conventions

Welcome to the World of Traits!

With the Write Traits® Classroom Kit, we offer you a way of teaching writing that helps students understand what good writing is and how to achieve it. The kit provides instruction in six traits of effective writing. The term *trait*, as it is used here, refers to a characteristic or quality that defines writing. The six traits of writing, as defined by teachers themselves, are these:

- Ideas
- Organization
- Voice
- Word Choice
- Sentence Fluency
- Conventions

Six-trait writing is based on the premise that students who become strong self-assessors become better writers and revisers, and we are quite certain that you will find this to be true. No matter where your student writers are right now, we are sure you will see improvements in their skills. You will also see them gain the confidence that comes from knowing writer's language and having options for revision.

Components in the Write Traits® Classroom Kit

Each *Write Traits Classroom Kit* contains the following components:

Teacher's Guide
The Teacher's Guide takes you step-by-step through each part of the program, from introducing the traits to presenting lessons to wrap-up activities that bring all traits together. Also contained in the Teacher's Guide are 6-point and 5-point reproducible rubrics and sample papers to practice scoring.

Student Traitbook
Available as a copymaster within the kit or for purchase for every student, the Student Traitbook contains all the practice exercises for the six traits.

Posters
Hang the two posters for students to use as a handy reference when revising their writing.

Self-stick Note Pads (package of 5)
Use these handy self-stick notes to indicate your scoring and comments so that you won't have to write directly on students' papers.

Overhead Transparencies
Use the transparencies for whole-class scoring or for discussion of the sample papers in the back of the Teacher's Guide.

Writing Pockets
Available for purchase for every student, this writing folder serves as a reminder to students of the six traits and as a place to store their writing in progress.

Teaching the Traits Units

The Teacher's Guide is organized into six units, one for each of the six traits. Each unit includes an overview, four lessons specifically designed to build strengths in that trait, and a unit wrap-up. At the end of the book are sample papers to use for practice in scoring papers.

Unit Overviews

Each of the six unit overviews accomplishes the following:

- defines the trait

- lists the instruction that will be emphasized

- provides a summary of each lesson

- contains two 6-point rubrics for scoring papers on the trait (one for the teacher, one for the student)

- recommends literature that can be used to model the trait

Traits Lessons

All twenty-four lessons, four for each of the six traits, follow the same format:

- Introduction, which includes an objective, skills focus, and suggested time frame

- Setting Up the Lesson, which introduces the main concepts of the lesson

- Teaching the Lesson, which provides teaching suggestions and answers for material in the Student Traitboook

- Extending the Lesson, which offers optional activities that carry the lesson concepts beyond the *Write Traits Classroom Kit*

Unit Summaries

Each of the six unit summaries does the following:

- reviews the characteristics of the trait
- looks at the rubric
- applies the rubric to scoring sample papers

Warm-up and Wrap-up Activities

Warm-up activities are provided to help you introduce the concept of traits *("What is a trait?")* and the concept of analyzing writing by allowing students to assess right from the start. Warm-up activities help students think like writers and heighten their awareness of the traits within writing samples. The wrap-up activities are designed to show you whether students have a full grasp of the traits and can use all six of them together.

Using Rubrics To Score Papers

Rubrics and Checklists

Please note that a checklist is NOT a rubric. The checklist included on your kit poster simply offers students a convenient way of reviewing their writing to be sure they have not forgotten any important elements of revision. The checklist includes no numbers and does not define performance at various levels along a rating scale. For this reason, neither you nor the students should use the checklist to assign scores.

Differences Between Rubrics

Our kit includes two 6-point rubrics for each trait, one for you and one for your students. We recognize that across the country, 4-, 5-, and 6-point scales are all in use. All have advantages. We believe, however, that the 6-point rubric reflects the greatest range of performance while still requiring raters to choose between generally strong papers (4s, 5s, or 6s) and papers in need of serious revision (1s, 2s, or 3s).

The 6-point scale allows the assigning of an "above expectations" score of 6. Further, it divides the midpoint portion of the scoring range into two scores: 3 and 4. Think of a score of 3 on a 6-point scale as a midrange performance, but one with a few more *weaknesses* than *strengths.* A score of 4, on the other hand, while also a midrange performance, has a few more *strengths* than *weaknesses.*

However, for your convenience we have also included 5-point rubrics, both teacher and student versions, in the appendix at the back of this Teacher's Guide.

Scoring Sample Papers

Sample papers included in this kit have been carefully selected to match precisely or very closely the grade level at which your students are writing. Some are informational; others are narrative. Some are well done; others reflect moderate to serious need for revision. These "in process" papers offer an excellent opportunity for students to practice revision skills on the work of others, and we recommend that you ask students to practice revising as many papers as time permits. This extended practice provides an excellent lead-in to the revision of their own work.

Suggested scores based on a 6-point scale are provided for each paper. (Scores based on the 5-point rubric are in the appendix.) These scores are just that—*suggestions*. They reflect the thoughtful reading and assessment of trained teachers, but they should not be considered correct "answers." While no score is final, any score must be defensible, meaning that the scorer can defend it using the language of the rubric.

Frequently Asked Questions

How did this six-trait approach get started?

The *Write Traits Classroom Kit* is based upon the six-trait model of writing instruction and assessment that teachers in the Beaverton, Oregon, School District developed in 1984. Because it has been so widely embraced by teachers at all grade levels, kindergarten through college, the model has since spread throughout the country—and much of the world. Traits themselves, of course, have been around as long as writing; writers have always needed intriguing ideas, good organization, a powerful voice, and so on. What is *new* is using consistent language with students to define writing at various levels of performance.

As a teacher, how can I make this program work for my students?

You can do several important things:

- Look to your students for answers; let them come up with their own ideas about what makes writing work, rather than simply giving them answers.

- Encourage students to be assessors and to verbalize their responses to many pieces of writing, including other students' work, professional writing, and your writing.

- Be a writer yourself, modeling steps within the writing process and encouraging students to use their increasing knowledge of the traits to coach you.

- Give students their own writing rubrics as you introduce each trait. Use the rubrics to assess writing and to help students see those rubrics as guides to revision.

- Share copies of rubrics with parents, too. This sharing encourages their involvement and helps them understand precisely how their children's writing is assessed.

Does six-trait instruction/assessment take the place of the writing process?

Absolutely not! The six-trait approach is meant to enhance and enrich a process-based approach to writing. Along with a wide set of options for revising, it gives students a language for talking and thinking like writers. Often students do not revise their writing thoroughly (or at all) because they have no idea what to do. Students who know the six traits have no difficulty thinking of ways to revise writing.

What do I do if I don't know a lot about the writing process?

Don't worry. We can help. First, you may wish to read the brief article by Jeff Hicks that summarizes the writing process. It appears on page xv of this Teacher's Guide and will give you all the basic information and terminology you need to work your way through the lessons without difficulty. If you would like to know more, refer to the Teacher Resources, page xviii. These resources will give you a strong background in the basics of the writing process, even if you've never been to a single workshop on the subject!

What do I have to give up from my current curriculum?

Nothing. If you are teaching writing through writers' workshops or any writing process-based approach, you will find that virtually everything you do is completely compatible with this program. It is ideally suited to process writing and particularly supports the steps of revision and editing.

Do I have to teach the traits in order?

We recommend that you teach both traits and lessons in the order presented because we use a sequential approach in which skills build on one another. Longer writing activities toward the end of each trait unit will require students to use the skills they have learned in studying a previous trait so that nothing is "lost." In other words, we do not want students to forget about *ideas* just because they move on to *organization.*

We do recognize, though, that most teachers prefer to teach conventions throughout the course of instruction, rather than as a separate unit. Therefore, incorporate instruction in conventions as you present the other traits.

Do all six traits ever come together?

Definitely. Writing should not be disjointed. We take it apart (into traits) to help students *master specific strategies for revision.* But eventually, we must put the slices of the pie back together. With this in mind, we provide several closure lessons, including one in which students will score a paper for all six traits and check their results with those of a partner. By this time, students will also be ready to assess and revise their own writing for all six traits. Wrap-up lessons may be assessed if you choose to do so.

Using Traits with the Writing Process

by Jeff Hicks

If writing were an act of fairytale magic or a matter of wishing, the word *process* would never apply to what people do when they write. All writers would have to do is wave their magic wands, rub their enchanted lamps to make their genies appear, or catch the one fish, from an ocean filled with fish, that grants wishes to the lucky person who hauls it in. *I'd like a bestseller about a pig and a spider who live on a farm. Allakazam! Presto! Newbery Medal!* Perhaps Roald Dahl was a fisherman and Beverly Cleary was a collector of antique lamps, right? Of course not! Writers understand that writing is a process involving multiple steps and plenty of time. An understanding of the process of writing is an important foundation for all young writers. Once they have the process in place, students can grasp and use the six traits of writing to help them revise and assess their own work. The six traits support the writing process.

The Writing Process The traditional view of the writing process is one that involves four or five steps or stages.

> **Prewriting**
> **Drafting (Writing)**
> **Revising**
> **Editing**
> **Publishing/Sharing**

1. **Prewriting**—This is the stage in which the writer attempts to find a topic, narrow it, and map out a plan. The writer usually isn't concerned with creating whole sentences or paragraphs at this point. Prewriting is done *before* the writer begins to write, and it is aimed at defining an idea and getting it rolling.

2. **Drafting** (Writing)—In this stage, the writer's idea begins to come to life. Sentences and paragraphs begin to take shape. The writer may experiment with different leads. In this stage, writers need to know that they can change directions, cross out words or sentences, and draw arrows to link details that are out of sequence. The term *rough draft*, or *first draft*, refers to writers in motion, changing directions and letting their ideas take shape.

3. **Revising**—When writers revise, their topics and ideas come into focus. In this stage, writers do a great deal of math—adding or subtracting single words, phrases, or entire paragraphs. What to revise often becomes clearer to students if they have had some time away from their drafts. Putting a draft away, out of sight and mind, for a few days or even more, may provide a sharper focus on weak areas. A writer might even ask, "Did I really write this?" The efforts made at revision will easily separate strong writing from weak writing.

4. **Editing**—This stage is all about making a piece of writing more accessible to readers. In this stage, writers fine-tune their work by focusing on correct punctuation, capitalization, grammar, usage, and paragraphing. Writers will want to be open to all the technological help (spell checker, for example) and human help they can find.

5. **Publishing/Sharing**—Not every piece of writing reaches this stage. The term *sharing* refers here to something more public than the kind of interactive sharing that should be happening at the previous stages. When writing is going to be "published" in the classroom or put on display as finished work, it needs to have been carefully selected as a piece of writing that has truly experienced all the other stages of the writing process.

These steps are often presented in classrooms as being separate, mutually exclusive events. *If I'm prewriting, I can't be revising. If I'm drafting, I can't be editing. If I'm revising, I can't be editing.* Mature writers know that the process may proceed through the steps in linear fashion, one at a time, but it is more likely that the parts of the process will intertwine. The process doesn't seem so overwhelming if a young writer can gain this perspective. I like to teach students several prewriting strategies—webbing, outlining, making word caches, drawing, and developing a list of questions—but I also like to show them through my own writing that prewriting and drafting can occur simultaneously. Having students experience their teacher as a writer is the most powerful way to demonstrate the importance of each stage and how it connects with the others. For instance, the best way for me to prewrite is to begin "writing." It is the act of writing (drafting) that often gets my ideas flowing better than if I tried to make a web of the idea. Writing also allows me to demonstrate that I can revise at any time. I can cross out a sentence, change a word, draw an arrow to place a sentence in a different paragraph, add a few words, or move a whole paragraph; all of this can be done while I draft an idea. At the same time, I might even notice that I need to fix the spelling of a word or add a period—that's editing!

Bringing in the Traits I know that many young writers speak and act as if they have magical pens or pencils. In the classroom, these are the students who proclaim, "I'm done!" minutes after beginning, or they are the ones who say, "But I like it the way it is!" when faced with a teacher's suggestion to tell a bit more or to make a few changes. Other students frequently complain, "I don't have anything to write about." Immersing these students in the writing process with a teacher who is also a writer is the clearest path to silencing these comments. Throw into this mix a strong understanding of the six traits of writing, and you are well on your way to creating passionate, self-assessing writers.

Teacher Resources
The "Must-Have" List for Teaching Writing Using the Six Traits

Ballenger, Bruce. 1993. *The Curious Researcher: A Guide to Writing Research Papers.* Needham Heights, MA: Allyn & Bacon.

Blake, Gary and Robert W. Bly. 1993. *The Elements of Technical Writing.* New York: Macmillan.

Calkins, Lucy McCormick. 1994. *The Art of Teaching Writing,* 2nd ed. Portsmouth, NH: Heinemann.

Fletcher, Ralph and Joann Portalupi. 1998. *Craft Lessons: Teaching Writing K–8.* Portland, Maine: Stenhouse Publishers.

Fox, Mem. 1993. *Radical Reflections: Passionate Opinions on Teaching, Learning, and Living.* New York: Harcourt Brace & Company.

Frank, Marjorie. 1995. *If You're Trying to Teach Kids How To Write . . . you've gotta have this book!* 2nd ed. Nashville: Incentive Publications, Inc.

Glynn, Carol. 2001. *Learning on Their Feet: A Sourcebook for Kinesthetic Learning Across the Curriculum K–8.* Shoreham, VT: Discover Writing Press.

Harvey, Stephanie. 1998. *Nonfiction Matters: Reading, Writing, and Research in Grades 3–8.* Portland, ME: Stenhouse Publishers.

Johnson, Bea. 1999. *Never Too Early to Write: Adventures in the K–1 Writing Workshop.* Gainesville, FL: Maupin House Publishing.

Lamott, Anne. 1994. *Bird by Bird: Some Instructions on Writing and Life.* New York: Doubleday.

Lane, Barry. 1998. *The Reviser's Toolbox.* Shoreham, VT: Discover Writing Press.

Murray, Donald M. 1985. *A Writer Teaches Writing.* 2nd ed. New York: Houghton Mifflin.

O'Conner, Patricia T. 1999. *Words Fail Me: What Everyone Who Writes Should Know About Writing.* New York: Harcourt Brace & Company.

Portalupi, Joann, with Ralph Fletcher. 2001. *Nonfiction Craft Lessons: Teaching Information Writing K–8.* Portland, Maine: Stenhouse Publishers.

Kemper, Dave, et al. 2000. *Writers Express.* Wilmington, MA: Great Source Education Group, Inc.

Spandel, Vicki. 2001. *Creating Writers,* 3rd ed. New York: Allyn & Bacon.

Spandel, Vicki, with Ruth Nathan and Laura Robb. 2001. *The Daybooks of Critical Reading and Writing.* Grades 3–5. Wilmington, MA: Great Source Education Group, Inc.

Stiggins, Richard J. 1996. *Student-Centered Classroom Assessment,* 2nd ed. Columbus, OH: Prentice Hall (Merrill).

Thomason, Tommy. 1998. *Writer to Writer: How to Conference Young Authors.* Norwood, MA: Christopher Gordon Publishers.

Thomason, Tommy and Carol York. 2000. *Write on Target: Preparing Young Writers to Succeed on State Writing Achievement Tests.* Norwood, MA: Christopher Gordon Publishers.

Using Write Traits Classroom Kits
with *Writers Express©*

Write Traits Classroom Kit, Grade 4	Skill Focus	*Writers Express* (Copyright© 2000)
Unit 1: Ideas		
Lesson 1: Getting Started	Gather details	Write Down Your Thoughts, p. 45
Lesson 2: What's Your Point?	Focus on main idea	Develop a Writing Plan, p. 47
Lesson 3: Thumbs Up, Thumbs Down	Choose interesting details	Adding Details, p. 83
Lesson 4: Unpacking to Stay in Focus	Delete unnecessary details	What Is Revising?, p. 56
Unit 2: Organization		
Lesson 5: Writing a Strong Lead	Write a lead	Writing a Lead, p. 163
Lesson 6: How Is It Organized?	Use organizational patterns	A Closer Look at the Parts [of a Paragraph], p. 77
Lesson 7: Matching the Pattern to the Task	Use organizational patterns	Putting Things in Order, p. 84
Lesson 8: Wrapping It Up	Write a conclusion	Writing the Ending, p. 53
Unit 3: Voice		
Lesson 9: Help! I Need a Voice-over!	Listen for voice	Modeling the Masters, p. 128
Lesson 10: Favorite Voices	Identify voice	Personal Voice, p. 21
Lesson 11: Pumping It Up!	Add details for voice	Show, Don't Tell, p. 58
Lesson 12: Your World, Your Voice	Develop personal voice	Writing a First Draft, p. 50

Unit 4: Word Choice		
Lesson 13: Verbs of Steel	Use strong verbs	Vivid Verbs, p. 127
Lesson 14: Using Context	Use context	Building Vocabulary Skills, pp. 288–294
Lesson 15: Painting Word Pictures	Use sensory language	Sensory Details, p. 127
Lesson 16: Pop That Balloon—Revise to Clarify	Cut out unnecessary words	Checking for Word Choice, p. 66
Unit 5: Sentence Fluency		
Lesson 17: Spice Up Your Sentences	Vary sentence beginnings	Checking for Smooth Sentences, p. 65
Lesson 18: Just Say No to Run-ons	Rewrite run-on sentences	Sentence Errors, p. 115
Lesson 19: Authentic Conversation	Write natural-sounding dialogue	Writing Dialogue, p. 215
Lesson 20: Read and Rank	Check for smoothness and flow	Combining Sentences, pp. 118–121
Unit 6: Conventions		
Lesson 21: What's the Difference?	Understand revising and editing	Revising, Editing, pp. 15, 16
Lesson 22: Reading the Signs	Use editor's marks	Editing and Proofreading Marks, p. 441
Lesson 23: The Eye and the Ear of the Editor	Edit text	Editing and Proofreading, pp. 64–67
Lesson 24: My Very Own Editing Checklist	Make an editing checklist	Editing and Proofreading Checklist, p. 67

Write Traits® Classroom Kit
SCOPE AND SEQUENCE

Trait/Skill	Grade					
	3	4	5	6	7	8
IDEAS						
Narrowing the Topic			•	•	•	•
Getting Started	•	•		•		•
Identifying the Main Idea	•	•	•			
Clarifying Ideas				•	•	•
Expanding Sketchy Writing			•	•	•	
Identifying What Is Important	•	•	•			
Making Writing Concise	•	•			•	•
ORGANIZATION						
Writing a Strong Lead	•	•	•			
Putting Things in Order	•		•		•	
Identifying Organizational Patterns		•		•		•
Matching Organizational Pattern and Writing Task		•		•		•
Staying on Topic	•		•		•	
Creating Strong Transitions				•	•	•
Writing Endings	•	•	•			
Putting Details Together				•	•	•
VOICE						
Defining Voice				•	•	•
Matching Voice and Purpose	•		•		•	
Putting Voice into Personal Narrative	•	•	•			
Putting Voice into Expository Writing				•	•	•
Matching Voice to Audience				•	•	•
Sharing Favorite Voices	•	•	•			
Putting Voice into Flat Writing		•		•		•
Using Personal Voice	•	•	•			

Trait/Skill	Grade					
	3	4	5	6	7	8
WORD CHOICE						
Using Strong Verbs	•	•	•			
Using Synonyms and Antonyms to Enhance Meaning				•	•	•
Inferring Meaning from Context	•	•	•			
Using Sensory Words to Create a Word Picture	•	•	•	•		•
Using Strong Words to Revise Flat Writing				•	•	•
Revising Overwritten Language		•		•	•	•
Eliminating Wordiness	•		•		•	
SENTENCE FLUENCY						
Making Choppy Writing Fluent	•		•		•	
Varying Sentence Beginnings	•	•				•
Varying Sentence Length			•	•	•	
Eliminating Run-ons	•	•		•		
Inserting Transitions				•	•	•
Creating Dialogue	•	•	•			
Assessing Fluency Through Interpretive Reading		•		•		•
Reading and Revising Personal Text			•		•	•
CONVENTIONS						
Distinguishing Between Revision and Editing		•	•	•	•	•
Spotting Errors	•		•	•		
Knowing the Symbols	•	•	•	•	•	•
Correcting Errors	•	•	•	•	•	•
Creating an Editing Checklist	•	•		•		•

Warm-Up Activities

Activity 1 is for trait beginners. If you and your students have worked with the six traits quite a bit already, you may wish to skip to Warm-up Activity 2. Warm-up Activity 1 should take about 10 minutes, Warm-up Activity 2 about 35 minutes.

Warm-Up Activity 1

"What Is a Trait?"

For use with Student Traitbook page 5

Start six-trait instruction with a definition of the term *trait,* which may be new to students. The word *trait* means *characteristic* or *quality* that helps define any concept, such as writing, reading, public speaking, cooking, and so on. In introducing this concept, encourage students to brainstorm the traits of something with which they are familiar, such as, a good hamburger or a good friend. This is, of course, just a warm-up for discussing the traits of good *writing,* but it helps plant the concept of *trait* in students' minds.

Ask students to brainstorm the qualities of *one or more* of the following (or anything from your own imagination):

- a good pet
- a good driver
- good weather

Write their responses on an overhead or on the chalkboard, and briefly discuss them. As you wrap up, make sure that the concept of *trait* is clear to everyone.

Now ask students to think of the qualities of good writing. This is another way of asking, "What makes writing work?" Encourage them to think about books that they have enjoyed and to tell what made the books enjoyable.

Again, write students' responses on the overhead or chalkboard and discuss them.

As a second step, if you think that students are ready, you might group responses that go together. For example, one student may say "It's organized," and another may say, "You can follow it." These concepts are closely connected, and the two ideas could be listed together. Similarly, "Spelling" and "Punctuation" go together because they are both part of editing. Do as much as you can to help students make these connections. This step will make it easier for them to see their own ideas reflected in the rubrics, when you use them trait by trait.

Ranking Three Papers

For use with Student Traitbook pages 5–6

This is an extended warm-up activity designed to help students begin working as assessors and thinking about what makes a piece of writing strong or weak. Students will not score these samples but will rank them from strongest to weakest and discuss their differences. In the discussions, you will probably hear the language of the traits even if you have not yet introduced them.

Have students turn to the three paragraphs that appear in the Student Traitbook on pages 5–6. As you will see, the descriptions differ primarily in quality and extent of detail, completeness of organizational structure, word choice, and voice. Conventions are quite strong in *all* examples because the purpose of the activity is to get students to think beyond conventions to other things that make writing work.

Tell students to make marks on the paragraphs as you read aloud or as they read silently. Suggest that students circle or underline parts that stand out because they are weak or strong. After reading or listening to each paragraph, students should use their marks to help them decide which paragraph is the strongest and which is the weakest. They should give reasons for ranking the papers in a particular way.

Ask students to share their rankings (record these on an overhead) and to explain their reasons briefly.

Rationales for Ranking

Students should see Sample 2 as the strongest. It has a more powerful voice, more detail, a better developed main idea (why my hometown is so appealing), and good word choice *(scary, flickering, gigantic).* By comparison, Samples 1 and 3 are very general. Sample 3 is somewhat stronger than Sample 1, which uses words like *neat* and *stuff* in place of solid detail. Sample 3 has some detail but does not begin to match Sample 2 in terms of what the reader can feel and picture. In addition, Sample 2 has a strong beginning and brings the whole piece to closure with the final lines. Sample 3 also has a clear (though brief) opening as well as a fair ending, though neither is as strong as the opening or ending in Sample 2. (**Note:** It is not necessary for students to make these precise observations; however, you should ask questions to prompt them in this general direction.)

Extensions

- Discuss what students would do to revise any of the three writing samples.

- Ask students to select one of the weaker samples (Sample 1 or Sample 3) and to revise it, using any details they like. Allow them to invent or delete information if they wish to do so.

- Ask each student to write a brief paragraph describing his or her hometown (or any other familiar place). Ask students to include as much detail as possible, modeling Sample 2. Share some paragraphs aloud.

- Make a chart of **Strengths** and **Problems.** List all the strengths and problems students notice for each of the three papers. Compare the lists. Do they show that students have ranked the papers appropriately?

WriteTraits®
TEACHER'S GUIDE

Overview

In this unit, students work with the concept of ideas—the writer's main message and all the details that support it. They will practice identifying main ideas, using prewriting strategies to plan, selecting details that enrich a main idea, and revising to eliminate filler (unneeded information). The purpose of this unit is to help students understand that good writing is dependent upon clear ideas that are well supported by quality details. Ideas are vital; this is the foundational trait within the six-trait model.

The focus of the instruction in this unit will be

- showing students how to use a variety of prewriting strategies.
- helping students focus on a main idea.
- modeling the difference between common details and the "treasures," or details that are unusual or interesting.
- showing students how to eliminate filler (unneeded information).

Ideas: A Definition

Ideas are the heart of any piece of writing. Ideas are all about information. In a strong creative piece, ideas paint a picture in the reader's mind. In an informational piece, strong ideas make difficult or complex information easy to understand. Good writing always makes sense. It always has a message or main point or story to tell. And it always includes carefully chosen details—those beyond-the-obvious bits of information that thoughtful, observant writers notice.

The Unit at a Glance

The following lessons in the Teacher's Guide and practice exercises in the Student Traitbook will help develop understanding of the trait of ideas. The Unit Summary provides an opportunity to practice evaluating papers for ideas.

Unit Introduction: Ideas

Teacher's Guide page 7
Student Traitbook page 7

Students are introduced to the unique features of the trait of ideas.

Lesson 1: Getting Started

Teacher's Guide pages 7–9
Student Traitbook pages 8–11

Students are introduced to one strategy for effective prewriting: building a list that includes significant details. After seeing how one writer puts this strategy to work, students will try it out for themselves.

Lesson 2: What's Your Point?

Teacher's Guide pages 10–12
Student Traitbook pages 12–15

Students are encouraged to focus on one main point and to stay with it; they also receive practice in using sketches as a prewriting technique.

Lesson 3: Thumbs Up, Thumbs Down

Teacher's Guide pages 13–15
Student Traitbook pages 16–19

Students learn to separate the interesting from the dull and tedious. Then they create a concise piece of writing that focuses on "Thumbs Up" details.

Lesson 4: Unpacking to Stay in Focus

Teacher's Guide pages 16–18
Student Traitbook pages 20–23

Students learn to "unpack" the filler from writing and recognize that filler adds weight, not interest.

Unit Summary: Ideas

Teacher's Guide page 19
Overhead numbers 1–4

Use the rubric on page 5 and the activities in the Summary to practice evaluating writing for ideas, details, and clarity.

Teacher Rubric for Ideas

6 ▪ The main ideas of the paper are clear. What the writer is trying to say is immediately obvious. The message or story is interesting—even memorable.
▪ The writer seems to have in-depth understanding of or insight about the topic, message, characters, and so on.
▪ The writer is selective, picking out unusual, beyond-the-obvious details that hold a reader's attention throughout the piece.

5 ▪ The paper makes sense from beginning to end. It is clear—never confusing.
▪ The writer knows enough about the topic to do a thorough job.
▪ The paper contains many interesting details.

4 ▪ Readers can identify the writer's main idea.
▪ The writer has some knowledge of the topic; more would enrich the paper.
▪ The writing includes some interesting or unusual details—enough to make the reader wish for more.

3 ▪ Readers can guess what the main idea is. Some parts are unclear, however, or do not seem to enhance the main idea or story.
▪ Sometimes the writer appears to know what he or she is talking about; at other times, the writer seems to search for things to say.
▪ Detail is present but minimal. Much of the writing consists of general statements that do little to expand the main message.

2 ▪ The main idea or story is hard to determine. The main point is unclear.
▪ The writer does not seem to know much about this topic and writes mainly to fill space.
▪ Details are sketchy or absent. The paper simply does not say much.

1 ▪ The writer is still searching for a main idea or story. The writing consists mainly of random thoughts or notes.
▪ The reader cannot extract anything meaningful.
▪ It is all but impossible to summarize this writing.

Student Rubric for Ideas

6
- The main idea of my paper is clear. It is easy to tell what I mean.
- I know a lot about this topic.
- My paper is full of interesting, unusual details that will keep readers reading.

5
- My paper makes sense. It is clear.
- I know quite a bit about this topic.
- My paper contains many interesting details.

4
- Readers can tell what my main idea is.
- I know some things about this topic. I wish I knew more.
- My writing has some interesting details. It could use more.

3
- Readers can probably guess what my main idea is. Some parts are not clear.
- I need more information. Sometimes I guessed or made things up.
- There is not much detail. It is mostly general statements.

2
- My main idea is hard to figure out. The reader may wonder what I am trying to say.
- I do not know much about this topic. Mostly I wrote to fill space.
- I need more details. My writing does not say much.

1
- I do not have a main idea. I wrote whatever came into my head.
- I am still figuring out what I want to say.
- None of this is clear. I do not think the reader will know what I am trying to say.

Recommended Literature for Teaching Ideas

Ask students to listen for details or main ideas, comment on details they recall, or pose questions about anything the author has not made clear.

Baylor, Byrd. 1986. *I'm in Charge of Celebrations*. New York: Aladdin Paperbacks. Excellent for helping students understand the importance of detail—noticing the little things.

Collard, Sneed B. III. *Creepy Creatures*. 1997. Watertown, MA: Charlesbridge Publishing. The unusual detail brought to life in nonfiction.

Edwards, Pamela Duncan. 1996. *Barefoot: Escape on the Underground Railroad*. New York: HarperCollins Publishers. Detail combined with realism, authenticity, and perspective. Great focus.

Fox, Mem. 1985. *Wilfrid Gordon McDonald Partridge*. New York: Kane/Miller Book Publishers. Exploring ideas through a question: What is a memory?

Jenkins, Steve. 1998. *Hottest, Coldest, Highest, Deepest*. New York: Houghton Mifflin Company. What's most important? Research for younger students.

Kemper, Dave with Ruth Nathan, Patrick Sebranek, and Carol Elsholz. 2000. *Writers Express: A Handbook for Young Writers, Thinkers, and Learners*. Wilmington, MA: Great Source. Writing process, writers' tips, connections to the six traits, forms of writing, proofreaders' guides—all the basics you need to bring the traits to life.

MacLachlan, Patricia. 1994. *All the Places to Love*. New York: HarperCollins Publishers. Personalizing detail to bring out voice.

Spandel, Vicki with Ruth Nathan and Laura Robb. 1994. *Daybook of Critical Reading and Writing* (Grade 4 edition). Wilmington, MA: Great Source. A marvelous collage of reading and writing activities based on the most exceptional literature of our time.

Getting Started

For use with pages 8–11 in the Student Traitbook

In this lesson, students learn the importance of planning and have an opportunity to practice one prewriting strategy: creating a list from image-building details. The emphasis is on helping writers develop a focus by using prewriting to connect main ideas to details.

Objectives

Students will gain skill in one form of prewriting: creating a list. Students will review prewriting and writing samples, create practice lists of their own, and write original paragraphs based on their lists.

Skills Focus

- Analyzing another writer's prewriting for use of detail
- Connecting another writer's prewriting sample to his writing sample
- Creating a prewriting list based on the **Who/Where/Doing** model
- Generating an original piece of text based on the prewriting list

Time Frame

Allow about 40 minutes for this lesson, which can be divided into two parts. Ask students to create a **Who/Where/Doing** prewriting list in Part 1 of the lesson (20 minutes). Then, in Part 2 of the lesson, ask them to write paragraphs using their lists. You may also have time for student partners to share their writing or for a few students to share with the whole class.

Setting Up the Lesson

Students may already have one or more ways to prepare for writing, the part of the writing process called *prewriting*. Ask what strategies they use to get started. Compare techniques by sharing your strategies, too. Here are some techniques to include on a list or a poster showing "Prewriting Strategies Our Class Uses":

- Thinking

- Talking to someone (including myself)

- Reading a book on my topic

- Drawing a picture

Accept any reasonable answer—the more variety the better. There is no *right answer* to the question, "What do you do when you prewrite?"

Teaching the Lesson

A Three-Part List: Building Images

Ask students to look carefully at the three-part list on Student Traitbook page 9 and circle any details they find especially interesting—details they hope to see included in the writer's story. You might also point out that this is a thorough list; the writer remembered many things. Still, he did not try to remember every single detail.

Use the List: "Adventures at the Rockpile"

Remind students to look back at the writer's list as they read the "Rockpile" paragraph. The important question here is "Did the list help the writer put together a good story?"

Was Anything Left Out?

An experienced writer will sometimes think of one or more new details while writing. Did that happen to this writer? (In other words, did the writer include anything that did not appear on the list?) Is this a good thing? Discuss with students their responses under "Was Anything Left Out?"

Choosing a Topic for Writing/ Make a Prewriting List

In this part of the lesson, students will be using the "Rockpile" writer's list and paragraph as models for creating first a list of their own and then a piece of writing based on that list. The "Rockpile" writer's list may seem extensive to some students, so encourage them to start small. Have students list one or two items in each column first; then have them see whether other ideas come to mind. The important point here is to have students include details that help a reader picture the people and the setting of the story. Remind students that writers make lists for themselves—not for others. So any notes they make should be useful to them in remembering and picturing.

Starting Your Paragraph

As students begin to write, remind them to use their lists as tools. They can borrow any ideas they wish, but they need not include every item on the list. Also, if they think of something interesting that is not on the list, they should feel free to include it, as long as it relates to the main topic.

Extending the Lesson

- Read aloud any passage of literature rich with detail, and ask students to brainstorm a "detail list" that the writer might have made before writing. (See page 6 of this Teacher's Guide.)

- Pick a topic. Ask students to help you create a detail list by asking questions. For example, your topic might be "My New Pet." Questions might include these: *What kind of pet is it? How did you get it? Do you like your pet? What is the hardest thing about caring for your pet?*

- On their next piece of writing, ask students to try a different prewriting technique: talking to someone, making a list of questions, drawing a picture and so on. Ask students to compare the two techniques they have used and tell which one worked best for them.

- Model one or more other forms of prewriting, such as doing a quick sketch, creating a word web or idea web, or reading a short passage. Be sure that you follow up your prewriting with a beginning draft so that students can see how your prewriting connects to your writing.

What's Your Point?

For use with pages 12–15 in the Student Traitbook

In this lesson, students identify the main idea in another writer's text and generate a piece of original writing in which the main idea and the supporting details are clear and strong.

Objectives

Students will learn to keep a main idea in focus when writing and to use details to support that main idea.

Skills Focus

- Understanding the concept of main idea
- Identifying the main idea—and recognizing the lack of a main idea
- Using a sketch to plan a piece of writing
- Writing a short paragraph based on a sketch

Time Frame

Allow about 40 minutes for this lesson. It can be broken into two parts. Part 1 includes analyzing Sample 1 and Sample 2 for the main idea and then setting up the writing "table sketch" in preparation for a piece of personal writing (20 minutes). Part 2 includes using the table sketch as a guide for generating a piece of original writing (20 minutes).

Setting Up the Lesson

Explain to students that a main idea is a message that the writer wishes to convey. Even when a writer stays with a single topic, he or she may still have no main idea. Consider the following sentences: *Blue flowers attract butterflies. There are many shades of blue. My eyes are blue. Sometimes the ocean is blue. Do you have a blue house? If you mix blue with yellow, it makes green.* These sentences share a topic—blue—but no main idea or message. Writing without a clear main idea or message is confusing.

Ask students to brainstorm the thoughts that come to mind when they hear the term *main idea.* Possible answers may include the bulleted ideas listed below. Record students' responses, and connect them to the concept of main idea.

- What the writer wants to say

- The most important thing the writer says

- The thing the writer talks about most

- What the writer wants the reader to understand

Teaching the Lesson

Finding the Main Idea

Students may need to read each paragraph on Student Traitbook pages 12–13 more than once. You may also wish to read either or both samples aloud if this is helpful.

Sample 1 is very scattered and has no main idea. It jumps from cakes to weddings to rice and bird seed—and then the environment. Most students should see this writing as confusing and out of focus. Sample 2, on the other hand, is focused. Students should see the writer's message clearly: *Weddings would be great if you did not have to wear such uncomfortable clothes!* Almost every sentence in the paragraph relates in some way to this main idea. You may wish to ask students whether they can find a single sentence that does not relate to the main idea. Discuss the results of their search.

Legs to Stand On

In this portion of the lesson, students use the sketch of a table to see that details support a main idea just as table legs support a tabletop. Discuss with students the way Sample 2 works with this model. Be sure the model is clear because students will use a table sketch for their own prewriting and writing activities.

Strong Legs ⟶ Strong Table

Remind students to look again at the table sketch done for Sample 2. They should notice how the details support the writer's main idea. This sketch then becomes a model for one of their own—based on a topic from the Student Traitbook or on a topic of their choice. Remind students that they need not fill in all four table legs (details). However, the fewer legs a table has, the harder it is for it to stand upright! In other words, writers may not need ten details, but one is probably not enough.

Remind students that sketching is a form of prewriting, or planning. By sketching out the table, they are making a plan for writing.

Writing from the Table

Students should use their sketches to create a short paragraph. Remind them to look carefully at the sketch as they work in order to remember important details. They also want to remain focused on the "tabletop"—that is, the main idea. When students share their writing, ask them to listen for main ideas and to be sure they can recognize a main idea in one another's writing.

Extending the Lesson

- Share a piece of your own writing, and see whether students can do a table sketch that would show your main idea and at least two or three supporting details.

- Share a piece of writing that has no clear main idea, and ask students to identify the main idea. Be sure to praise them if they tell you that there is no main idea.

- Discuss differences between the two prewriting strategies you have used in this unit: listing (from Lesson 1) and sketching the table (from Lesson 2). Which was more helpful? Students may disagree on this because different writers choose different paths into writing.

Thumbs Up, Thumbs Down

For use with pages 16–19 in the Student Traitbook

In this lesson, students use the "thumbs up, thumbs down" concept to consider which details are critical to a piece of writing and which can be discarded.

Objectives

Students will understand that unnecessary details add neither interest nor value. They will recognize important information and use it to make their writing more concise *and* engaging.

Skills Focus

- Identifying interesting information
- Writing a short paragraph that focuses on intriguing details

Time Frame

Allow about 30 minutes for this lesson.

Setting Up the Lesson

For a class activity, ask students to select a topic in which they are interested—pets, friends, movies, video games, and so on. Then ask them to imagine that they are writing papers on this topic for readers who know very little about it and perhaps have no interest in it. The challenge is to make the topic engaging. Ask students to brainstorm details that readers would enjoy hearing about. When the list is complete, have them go back over it and choose the *top six details.* Discuss what makes some details more interesting than others.

> *Growing up with five brothers taught me that it's good to be the guy telling the story after the lamp gets broken.*
>
> —Jon Scieszka, author

Teaching the Lesson

Sorting It Out: THUMBS UP or DOWN?

Students may need to read the list more than once. They should go through it fairly quickly, asking, "Is this interesting? Would I like to hear more about this?" Remind students that it is NOT necessary to know anything about the country of Saudi Arabia in advance. In fact, it may be helpful if some of your students know very little about it. They will respond to the details with a fresh perspective, thinking only about what interests them.

Compare Lists

Allow two to three minutes for pairs of students to compare the details that each partner circled. Using these comparisons, students can add or subtract check marks if they wish.

Using the THUMBS UP! to Write

When students have identified the most interesting pieces of information from the Saudi Arabia list and have compared their choices with those of a partner, they may write. Before they begin, suggest that they count the number of details they have selected. There are many details on this list; using all of them would result in a very long paper. Suggest that they work to cut the list in half. Eight or ten details will probably work well but this means cutting a lot of material. Are they up to the job? Are *you?* Make your own list of interesting details and write from it. Do not share your writing until students have shared theirs.

Extending the Lesson

- Ask students to share their THUMBS UP! paragraphs—and share yours, too. Discuss the different details students selected as being of interest.

- Ask students to try the same exercise, but this time they are to imagine that they are writing to *students in first grade.* Would their selection of details change? Would they choose a smaller list?

- Invite students to review a piece of writing from their writing folders. Suggest that they put a check mark (or another indicator) next to each THUMBS UP! detail they find. Are there many? Could there—*should* there—be more? Discuss what students should do about adding details to their work.

Unpacking to Stay in Focus

For use with pages 20–23 in the Student Traitbook

Getting rid of unnecessary information is one of a writer's most difficult jobs. Sometimes it's easier to "tell everything" than to decide what information should be cut. This lesson builds on Lesson 3 (selecting interesting details) by showing students how to revise for conciseness after a draft has been written. Students will first see how a skilled writer keeps her story concise and then have an opportunity to revise to eliminate unnecessary details.

Objectives

Students will expand on skills learned in Lesson 3, "unpacking" overloaded writing by identifying and deleting unnecessary material.

Skills Focus

- Understanding that length must be adjusted to purpose and audience
- Identifying filler in a piece of written text
- Being a reviser/editor: removing filler from another's writing
- Recognizing and removing filler found in one's own text

Time Frame

Allow about 35 minutes for this lesson.

Setting Up the Lesson

Filler is irrelevant information that does nothing to explain or enrich the idea. It could be information that everyone knows: *cars run on gas, dentists work on teeth, many people have pets.* Readers usually find filler distracting and confusing. For example, a reader who is finding out how watches are made does not want to be brought into a discussion of how beautiful leaves are in the fall.

Explain that students will be looking at and listening to two very different pieces of writing. In each case, they will be looking and listening for filler. As they read and listen, they should be asking themselves, "Is this writer giving me new information? Is this helpful or interesting information? Does it have anything to do with the writer's main idea?"

Teaching the Lesson

Sharing an Example: Dovey Coe
Read the paragraph on Student Traitbook pages 20–21 aloud. Ask for responses: What did they like about the paragraph? Was there anything they did not understand? Then ask them to focus on details. What specific details do they recall? After students have identified some specific details, have them reread the excerpt.

What Did You Find Out?
This is an opportunity for students to find interesting details and to suggest the unimportant details the writer deliberately leaves out. In the circle for unnecessary details, students should list items such as the following:

- How much Dovey weighs
- What color Dovey's eyes are
- Dovey's mother's name
- Where Dovey was born

Explain that these details weigh a piece of writing down like a sack full of rocks in the river. If students don't want their writing to sink, they should leave out the unnecessary information!

What If?

In this portion of the lesson, look carefully at the example about Nico. Do students agree with the way this reviser took out filler? Would they have taken out the same line? Why or why not?

Finding the Filler

This portion of the lesson is the most challenging. The paragraph on Student Traitbook page 22 is fairly long, and it contains *a lot* of filler. Make a transparency of the paragraph if you wish to work on it as a class. Here is a suggested revision, with filler crossed out:

Winter is my favorite season. The only problem is, we haven't had a real winter for at least two years, so we haven't had much snow. When it snows, I can sled, build forts, and have snowball fights. ~~Did you see that movie called *Snowday*? If it snows very hard, they cancel school for at least a day. I do like recess at school. I get tired of just sitting at my desk all the time.~~ After a big snowfall, my friends all meet in my yard, where we build a huge snowman. We have to lift my little sister up on our shoulders so she can put the hat on the snowman's head. ~~She just got a new coat for her birthday.~~ I guess if I want real winter, I will have to get my parents to move to Minnesota or Maine or Alaska, where winter lasts almost forever. ~~I did a report on Wisconsin once. They have pretty cold winters, and they make a lot of cheese there. I love cheese.~~

Share and Compare

Talking about writing is important, so allow time for students to compare their revised versions with those of their partners.

Extending the Lesson

- Write a short paragraph to which you deliberately add a lot of filler. Then ask students to help you revise it by cutting what is not needed.

- Ask students to check a passage from a textbook. Do they find any filler, or did the writer do a good job of taking it out?

- Ask each student to write a short paragraph in which he or she intentionally adds some filler. The paragraph should be at least six sentences long, and at least two of the sentences should be filler. Then have each student trade paragraphs with a partner and revise to make the writing concise. Students may then share their paragraphs with the class. Share one or two aloud. Be sure students check their current writing for filler and revise as necessary.

Ideas

Teacher's Guide pages 5, 118–129
Overhead numbers 1–4

Objectives

Students will review and apply what they have learned about the trait of ideas.

Reviewing Ideas

Review with students what they have learned about the trait of ideas. Ask students to discuss what ideas are and to explain why they are important in a piece of writing. Then ask them to recall the main points about ideas that are discussed in Unit 1. Students' responses should include the following points:

- Use prewriting activities to prepare for writing.
- Focus on a main idea.
- Use interesting details to add interest.
- Take out clutter or unnecessary details.

Applying Ideas

To help students apply what they have learned about the trait of Ideas, distribute copies of the Student Rubric for Ideas on page 5 of this Teacher's Guide. Students will use these to score one or more sample papers that can be found beginning on page 115. The papers for ideas are also on overhead transparencies 1–4.

Before students score the papers, explain that a rubric is a grading system to determine the score a piece of writing should receive for a particular trait. Preview the Student Rubric for Ideas, pointing out that a paper very strong in ideas receives a score of 6, and a paper very weak in ideas receives a score of 1. Tell students to read the rubric and then to read the paper to be scored. Then tell them to look at the paper and the rubric together to determine the score the paper should receive. Encourage students to make notes on each paper to help them score it. For example, they might put a check mark next to an interesting detail or draw a line through useless or irrelevant information.

Organization

Overview

In this unit, students study the concept of organization, the way a writer orders ideas. You can think of organization as the internal construction of a building—the part that holds up the walls —or as the skeleton of an animal. Organization does not show on the surface, but without it the whole work would come apart.

The focus of the instruction in this unit will be
- working with students on recognizing and writing strong leads.
- introducing three organizational patterns that fit a particular purpose for writing.
- talking about the importance of matching organizational pattern to the purpose for writing and the audience.
- working with students on recognizing and writing strong conclusions.

Organization: *A Definition*

Organization is about the logical and effective presentation of key ideas and details. Good organization keeps a piece of writing together and makes it easy to follow—like good instructions or a clear road map. The purpose for the writing affects organization strongly. For example, in a business letter, good organization might call for coming to the point quickly, getting through the main ideas efficiently, and bringing the letter to a quick conclusion. The organization of a mystery story might call for the writer to keep some ideas hidden for a time, so that the reader can guess what will happen. The writer may also linger over descriptions of character or setting.

The Unit at a Glance

The following lessons in the Teacher's Guide and practice exercises in the Student Traitbook will help develop understanding of the trait of organization. The Unit Summary provides an opportunity to practice evaluating papers for organization.

Unit Introduction: Organization

Teacher's Guide page 25
Student Traitbook page 24

Students are introduced to the unique features of organization.

Lesson 5: Writing a Strong Lead

Teacher's Guide pages 25–27
Student Traitbook pages 25–28

Students listen to a professional writer's lead, select the stronger lead for a piece of writing from two choices, and create good leads of their own.

Lesson 6: How Is It Organized?

Teacher's Guide pages 28–30
Student Traitbook pages 29–32

Students look at three organizational patterns and match the pattern to an actual piece of writing. Each student then chooses one pattern to imitate and writes an original paragraph based on that pattern.

Lesson 7: Matching the Pattern to the Task

Teacher's Guide pages 31–33
Student Traitbook pages 33–36

Students build on skills gained through Lesson 6 by learning three more organizational patterns and matching patterns to writing tasks. Students then create original pieces of writing, selecting patterns they think will work best.

Lesson 8: Wrapping It Up

Teacher's Guide pages 34–36
Student Traitbook pages 37–40

Students listen to an effective conclusion, talk about what makes conclusions work, choose an appropriate conclusion for an unfinished story, and create conclusions of their own.

Unit Summary: Organization

Teacher's Guide page 37
Overhead numbers 5–8

Use the rubric on page 23 and the activities in the Summary to practice evaluating writing for organization.

Teacher Rubric for Organization

6
- The writer stays focused on the main point.
- The organizational pattern correctly matches the topic, purpose, and audience.
- The lead is engaging, and the conclusion is thoroughly satisfying.

5
- The writer seldom wanders from the main point.
- The organizational pattern fits the topic, purpose, and audience.
- The lead is appealing, and the conclusion works well.

4
- The writer may meander briefly, but the writing is not distracting or confusing.
- The organizational pattern works most of the time.
- The lead and conclusion are unoriginal but functional.

3
- The writer wanders from the main point enough to make the piece confusing.
- The organizational pattern is not a good match for this topic, purpose, or audience. It may be too formulaic, or the writer does not follow a pattern.
- The lead and the conclusion are present; one or both need work.

2
- Lack of order frequently leaves the reader confused.
- The formulaic pattern is distracting—or there is no pattern.
- The lead and the conclusion are missing or need a lot of work.

1
- The text is a disjointed collection of random thoughts.
- No identifiable structure or pattern exists. The writing is impossible to follow.
- The lead and the conclusion are missing.

Student Rubric for Organization

6
- My paper is easy to follow. I never wander from the topic.
- My organizational pattern fits my topic, purpose, and audience.
- My lead grabs attention, and my conclusion sounds just right.

5
- My paper is easy to follow. I stick with one topic—*most* of the time.
- My organizational pattern fits my topic, purpose, and audience.
- My lead is very good, and my conclusion is good, too.

4
- My paper is pretty easy to follow. I might have wandered a little from my main topic.
- I have an organizational pattern. I think it fits my purpose. I followed it most of the time.
- My lead is OK, and my conclusion is OK, too.

3
- My paper is a little hard to follow. I wandered from my main topic now and then.
- I tried to follow an organizational pattern. It might not go with my purpose.
- I have a lead and a conclusion, but I do not like either of them.

2
- My paper is hard to follow—I wrote about too many things, and I forgot what my main topic was.
- I do not see a pattern here. This is more like a messy closet.
- I think I forgot to write a lead and a conclusion.

1
- This is just a bunch of ideas. No one could follow it.
- This doesn't make any sense. I don't even *have* a main topic yet.
- Pattern? Are you kidding? Nothing goes with anything else.
- I have no lead or conclusion.

Additional Recommended Books for Teaching Organization

Use excerpts from these books or from your favorites to model leads, organizational patterns, or conclusions.

Dahl, Roald. 1991. *The Twits.* New York: Puffin Books. Excellent lead and conclusion. Also, first part of book can be used to show comparison-contrast between Mr. and Mrs. Twit.

DiCamillo, Kate. 2000. *Because of Winn-Dixie.* Cambridge, MA: Candlewick Press. Exceptional lead and conclusion. Chronology is the main pattern, but main ideas emerge and flourish.

Fox, Mem. 1989. *Feathers and Fools.* New York: Harcourt Brace and Company. Superb lead and conclusion. Excellent illustration of comparison-contrast organization, combined with chronology.

Kemper, Dave with Ruth Nathan, Patrick Sebranek, and Carol Elsholz. 2000. *Writers Express.* Wilmington, MA: Great Source. Many ideas on organizing information well across multiple forms of writing.

Nye, Bill. 1993. *Bill Nye the Science Guy's Big Blast of Science.* New York: Addison-Wesley. Excellent organization of informational writing: key points, main idea and support, big idea to little idea, comparison-contrast.

Palatini, Margie. 1995. *Piggie Pie.* New York: Clarion Books. Zany, hilarious lead and conclusion.

Paulsen, Gary. 1999. *Canoe Days.* New York: Bantam Doubleday Dell Publishing. Wonderful illustration of key ideas building to a larger theme.

Spandel, Vicki with Ruth Nathan and Laura Robb. 2001. *The Daybook of Critical Reading and Writing* (Grade 4). Wilmington, MA: Great Source. Excellent samples of a variety of organizational patterns. Connects reading and writing.

More Ideas

Looking for more ideas on using literature to teach organization? We recommend *Books, Lessons, Ideas for Teaching the Six Traits: Writing in the Elementary and Middle Grades,* published by Great Source. Compiled and annotated by Vicki Spandel. For information, please phone 800-289-4490.

Writing a Strong Lead

For use with pages 25–28 in the Student Traitbook

In this lesson, students learn that while there is no single right way to craft a lead, some leads are much better than others at grabbing and holding a reader's attention. A good lead "stirs up" a reader's curiosity and keeps the reader engaged.

Objectives

Students will identify and write strong leads.

Skills Focus

- Listening to a professional writer's lead to learn how to write effective leads
- Choosing the better of two leads
- Writing original leads and working with a partner to distinguish between strong and weak leads

Time Frame

Allow 40 minutes for this lesson. You can divide the lesson into two parts, if you wish. Part 1 (20 minutes) includes listening to and discussing the opening lead and selecting the stronger lead for each of two stories. Part 2 (20 minutes) includes writing original leads and sharing them with partners.

Setting Up the Lesson

Before beginning the lesson, make sure that every student knows that an effective lead sets the stage, hints at what is coming, and captures the reader's interest. A lead may be one sentence or many.

Throughout this unit on organization, continue to share books with strong leads and conclusions. Talk about what makes each one work. If you find samples of writing from any source (advertisements, brochures, newspaper articles, and so on) with weak leads or conclusions, share those, too. Talk about how they could be made stronger.

Teaching the Lesson

Sharing an Example: The Bad Beginning

Read aloud the lead on Student Traitbook page 26, asking students to follow along. The lead is strong in voice and so can be read with great expression. In addition, it invites wonderful predictions about what may happen.

Encourage students to write down any responses they have to this lead. Have them explain whether they like it, why it works or does not work, any predictions they have, and so on. Share responses in a class discussion.

Choosing a Winner

In this part of the lesson, students choose the stronger lead for each of two stories—one about a wolf, the other about pioneers. From the possible leads for a story about a wolf, most students should select option A. It is lively, engaging, and full of possibilities. The idea of Mantak being alone—perhaps lost or in danger—piques our curiosity. Lead B is dull and uneventful. It tells facts, but builds no curiosity in readers.

Of the possible leads for a report on Oregon Trail pioneers, lead B is the clear choice. This lead makes the pioneers sound adventurous, daring, and spirited. Lead A makes them sound as if they were loaded into the wagons like freight. It has no life, no voice, no energy or excitement. The writer sounds bored, and we are, too. However, some students may prefer the weaker lead. If this happens, have them explain the reasons behind their choices, and encourage other students to join the discussion.

Your Turn at Bat

Surprisingly, writing intentionally bad can be enlightening. Encourage your students to have fun as they write their weak leads. On the other hand, they should work hard on their good leads to create an opening that will hook readers. Many books go unread because the leads do not attract readers. Be sure that students read their leads aloud to each other and share with the class as well.

Extending the Lesson

- Ask students to look at any piece of writing on which they are currently working. Ask them to write two or more new leads for these pieces, and then share them in a writing group. Which leads do the groups like best?

- Ask each student to bring in a favorite book. In writing groups, ask them to share the leads and to vote for favorites within the group. Read group favorites aloud to the class.

- Read several leads from the local paper. Try for some variety—headline news, sports, entertainment, and so on. Ask students to do a "thumbs up" or "thumbs down" vote on each lead to indicate whether they would keep reading. In each case, they should explain their reasoning.

- Choose one of the topics from the list, or make up one of your own. Write two strong leads and two weak leads on an overhead transparency, on chart paper, or on the board. Ask students to identify the leads by type and explain why they are weak or strong. After they have finished, let them know if you agree.

How Is It Organized?

For use with pages 29–32 in the Student Traitbook

This lesson is about patterns in writing. The term *pattern* refers to the kind of organizational structure the writer has chosen to present his or her ideas in the clearest, most compelling fashion. Cause-and-effect might be one pattern, comparison-contrast another, chronological order another. This is a lesson of exploration, but it also allows students an opportunity to write and to see whether they can follow a model.

Objectives

Students will learn to recognize three organizational patterns in short pieces of writing and use one pattern as a model for their own writing.

Skills Focus

- Listening for the pattern in a piece of professional writing
- Understanding three organizational patterns: step-by-step, comparison-contrast, and most important to least important
- Identifying the pattern in each of three pieces of writing
- Creating an original piece of writing, using one of the three patterns as a model

Time Frame

Allow about 30 minutes for this lesson.

Setting Up the Lesson

In this lesson, students will be looking at three different organizational patterns and talking about which one best fits the writer's purpose. This list of three is not comprehensive; it's a beginning point.

Discuss with students that in a piece of writing, the term *pattern* refers to the way the writing is put together: a recipe is put together in ordered steps; a comparison of two presidential candidates is put together by description. When a piece of writing is clear, readers can tell what the basic pattern is. Let students know that their job in this lesson is "seeing" (or "hearing") the pattern within the writing.

Teaching the Lesson

Sharing an Example: *Ira Sleeps Over*

Read aloud the excerpt on Student Traitbook pages 29–30, asking students to think about the pattern in the writing as you read. Give them some hints: Is it a comparison paper? Does it make one main point and then give support? Or does it give step-by-step information? If students have some idea of what to listen for, it is easier to hear the step-by-step pattern in this passage.

Three Organizational Patterns

Students are introduced to three organizational patterns: *step-by-step, comparison-contrast,* and *most important to least important*. Take time to go through each pattern, making sure students understand how each works. You might ask whether they can think of examples of step-by-step, comparison-contrast, or most important to least important organization.

Naming the Pattern

Students should find this fairly simple *if* they understand the patterns presented. If these patterns are not clear, this portion of the lesson will be difficult. Students can certainly read these samples on their own, but if they get stuck, it may be helpful for you to read one or more samples aloud and ask them to listen for the pattern they hear. For example, if students were to choose comparison-contrast for Sample 1, you might read the sample aloud and then ask, "What two things are being compared?" Clearly, this pattern does not fit.

Students should make these choices: Sample 1 (most important to least important), Sample 2 (step-by-step), and Sample 3 (comparison-contrast). Explain any sample students find difficult, and point out why the pattern fits.

Imitating a Pattern

Here students will do some writing on their own. Encourage them to pick a pattern with which they feel comfortable. Students may choose a pattern they like, and the pattern may help suggest a topic. Help them start by choosing a pattern yourself and then choosing a topic that will model the pattern. For example, you might decide to do a step-by-step (or how-to) paper, and then explain that you are going to write "How to Make Never-Fail Spaghetti." Explain why the pattern you chose fits your topic. Write a paragraph that you will share later, but do not let students see what you write until they have written their own paragraphs. You may wish to ask for a show of hands on the patterns chosen to encourage some variety. Encourage each student to share his or her paragraph with a partner.

Extending the Lesson

- Ask students to look at any piece of writing on which they are currently working to see whether they can identify a pattern. It need not be one of the patterns you talked about in this lesson.

- Model any pattern students do not feel comfortable with by writing a short paragraph (about five sentences) on an overhead transparency, on chart paper, or on the board.

- Choose a piece of writing that has a clear organizational pattern (a set of instructions is good) and ask students to identify the pattern by listening to the selection read aloud.

Matching the Pattern to the Task

For use with pages 33–36 in the Student Traitbook

Not all pieces of writing fit all patterns. For example, it wouldn't make much sense to write a recipe as a comparison-contrast piece: *Roasting a turkey is different from baking a pie—though you need utensils and an oven for both.* Writers must be clear not only about what they want to tell but about how they plan to structure it.

Objectives

Students will match an organizational pattern with the writing task at hand so that information is presented in a clear and inviting way.

Skills Focus

- Understanding six patterns of writing (including the three presented in Lesson 6)
- Matching an appropriate organizational pattern to a given writing task
- Creating an original piece of writing in one of the six patterns

Time Frame

Allow about 35 minutes for this lesson.

Setting Up the Lesson

Remind students that the organizational pattern of a piece of writing must match the purpose. Otherwise, the writing will sound odd and disorganized. Give students an example. Ask them to listen to both versions of a description of a garden, and have them decide which description makes more sense.

1. *First, look at the carrots. Now, look at the onions. Third, notice the flowers. Finally, look carefully at the big shade trees. Before leaving, notice the colors and smells. . . .*

2. *The main thing you will notice about my garden is that it is very peaceful, with many soft colors and the sound of birds. Second, you will notice a large variety of plants—everything from vegetables to giant trees. Finally, if you have a sensitive nose, you may notice many different smells, from onions to roses. . . .*

Which description is easier to follow? The first example has a step-by-step organization that works well for recipes and directions, but not for this description. The pattern in the second example moves from the most important point to the least important point. It seems to work better.

Teaching the Lesson

Six Patterns: Organizing Your Writing

This portion of the lesson allows students to expand their ability to organize. The list of six patterns on Student Traitbook page 34 includes the three from Lesson 6 as well as three more: *main idea and support, chronological retelling,* and *key points* (which could be based on readers' questions). Be sure to go over this list with students point by point. The idea is to understand that there are many ways to organize writing, and the way they choose depends on their purpose. Remind them that they can refer to the list at any time.

Playing Matchmaker

In this part of the lesson, students match the pattern to the task. They will be working as partners, so suggest that the pairs discuss how each piece of writing could be organized. Also remind them that there could be more than one way to organize a piece of writing and that there are likely to be some ways that do not work well. A chronological retelling might be just right for a newspaper story about a bank robbery. A key points approach could work, too. On the other hand, comparing the bank robbery to other robberies is probably not the most effective way to present the facts.

Compare with the Class

Discuss choices with the entire class after students have matched the patterns to the tasks.

Using a Pattern

To close this lesson, have each student choose one of the patterns and write a paragraph that is essentially an advertisement. Several patterns will fit this paragraph: key points, comparison, most important point to least important point, and main idea with support. Even chronology could be used if a clever writer chose to provide readers with, for example, the "history of the yo-yo." Remind students to think of the message first. Ask questions like these: *What do you want to say? Which pattern will let you say it?*

Extending the Lesson

- Read aloud as many of the advertisement paragraphs as time permits. Have students listen for organizational patterns. Notice whether students choose different patterns to do the same kind of assignment.

- Have students look for patterns in any short pieces of reading done for this class. Tell them not to worry about whether the pattern they see matches one of the six in this lesson. Have them identify the pattern the writer used to put information into logical order.

Wrapping It Up

For use with pages 37–40 in the Student Traitbook

A good conclusion puts the finishing touch on a piece of writing. Conclusions have a sound and feel all their own, and it's a sound and feel that takes practice to sense. Most students will need to read and hear conclusions for some time before this process becomes familiar to them. This lesson is a beginning. It offers time to reflect on what makes a conclusion work and why some conclusions are more effective than others.

Objectives

Students will differentiate between strong and weak conclusions and be able to write effective conclusions.

Skills Focus

- Identifying qualities of a strong conclusion through listening and discussion
- Choosing the strongest of three conclusions for a piece of writing
- Drafting a conclusion for an unfinished piece of writing

Time Frame

Allow 30–40 minutes for this lesson. The lesson can be divided into two parts. In Part 1 (20 minutes) students will listen to and discuss the *Shiloh* conclusion and then select the best conclusion for the story called "Mantak." In Part 2 (20 minutes), students will read and draft a conclusion for the story called "Take Me to Your Leader."

Setting Up the Lesson

Discuss with students that a *conclusion* is an ending, yet it's also more than just the final line of an essay or story. A conclusion leaves the reader with a sense of satisfaction and completeness. Discuss the importance of good conclusions. Read several of your favorite conclusions from any literature in your class (See the list of recommended books on page 24 of this Teacher's Guide.) Ask students to state specifically what they like or do not like about each conclusion. If you have time, also read aloud some conclusions from encyclopedia entries or textbook chapters. Some may be *very* well done. Others may lack the qualities of a good conclusion. Talk about what's missing.

Teaching the Lesson

Sharing an Example: *Shiloh*
The passage on Student Traitbook page 37 has that "just right" ending kind of sound. Ask students whether they think the story is over. Would it be odd if the narrator went on? (for example, *So the next day, Shiloh and I had this other adventure. . . .*) Any time it feels wrong to go on, you can be sure you've hit on a good conclusion.

Select an Ending: "Mantak"
Let students read "Mantak" on their own, if possible. If any students struggle with it, you can read aloud as they follow along. Make sure students understand the essentials of the story, so that they can determine what kind of ending works best. Is this a happy story? Sad? Scary? What is Mantak's main problem right now? Do you think she will solve it? How is she feeling about her life now?

What's Your Choice?
Most students are likely to choose conclusion 2. This is the strongest conclusion of the three choices. It depicts Mantak as brave despite her troubles. She is "Ruler of the night." What a great last line. That's a wrap-up for you; it helps us predict what will happen.

By contrast, look at conclusion 1. It is factual and general. The line "She had learned a great deal" does not tell us much about Mantak or her situation. The writer sounds tired.

Conclusion 3 starts out with some interest. Poor Mantak is still bleeding, and could be hunted by other predators. But it sounds as if the writer was in a hurry to finish because suddenly Mantak makes friends with a bear. Is this believable? Some students may choose this option for its "happily ever after" sound. But not all good stories end with all problems solved.

Your Turn to Write

Before they write, ask students to think again about some of the conclusions you have shared. Ask them, "What should a good conclusion do?" or "How should a good conclusion sound?" Then ask them to write. Encourage students to write more than one conclusion and to choose the favorite. Ask each student to imagine that this is the conclusion to a novel he or she hopes to sell. How good it is might determine whether anyone will buy the next book.

Extending the Lesson

- Share your own conclusion for "Take Me to Your Leader." Ask students to do a critique of your work.

- Ask a volunteer to write (for you) a practice story with no conclusion. Tell students you will draft the conclusion on the overhead in front of the class. They can also try their hands at writing a conclusion for the same paper. Then all of you can share.

- Ask whether anyone would like to write an alternate conclusion for "Mantak." Allow at-home time for this. Then, read results aloud.

Organization

Teacher's Guide pages 23, 130–141
Overhead numbers 5–8

Objectives

Students will review and apply what they have learned about the trait of organization.

Reviewing Organization

Review with students what they have learned about the trait of organization. Ask students to discuss what organization means and to explain why it is important in a piece of writing. Then ask them to recall the main points about organization that are discussed in Unit 2. Students' responses should include the following points:

- Begin with a strong lead.
- Use the right structure for the audience and purpose.
- Finish with a strong conclusion.

Applying Organization

To help students apply what they have learned about organization, distribute copies of the Student Rubric for Organization on page 23 of this Teacher's Guide. Students will use these to score one or more sample papers that can be found beginning on page 115. The papers for organization are also on overhead transparencies 5–8.

Before students score the papers, explain that a rubric is a grading system to determine the score a piece of writing should receive for a particular trait. Preview the Student Rubric for Organization, pointing out that a paper that is well organized receives a score of 6, and a paper that is not organized receives a score of 1. Tell students to read the rubric and then to read the paper to be scored. Then tell them to look at the paper and the rubric together to determine the score the paper should receive. Encourage students to make notes on each paper to help them score it. For example, they might put a check mark next to a strong lead or conclusion and an *X* next to a weak lead or conclusion.

Overview

In this unit, students explore the concept of voice, the way in which a writer lets his or her personality and perspective shine through the writing. Voice is part individuality, part energy and feeling, and part audience connection. It's a complex trait, but a vital one—without it, writing can be painfully dull.

The focus of the instruction in this unit will be

- helping students develop an "ear" for voice.
- providing opportunities for students to recognize different voices.
- showing students how to revise to include feelings, details, and sensory language.
- encouraging students to develop a strong voice.

Voice: *A Definition*

Voice has sometimes been called "the fingerprints of the writer on the page." As one teacher put it, ideas are what you have to say; voice is how you say it. Voices are distinctive and tend to become more so as writers practice their craft and become increasingly aware of their own personal voice. It would be difficult to mistake the voice of Jerry Seinfeld for the voice of Carl Sagan or Maya Angelou or Byrd Baylor. Voices are unique and also change with purpose. The voice of a business letter is different from the voice in a letter to a friend or the voice in a story about a scary experience. Yet if Byrd Baylor wrote all three of these, there would be something of *her* in each piece.

The Unit at a Glance

The following lessons in the Teacher's Guide and practice exercises in the Student Traitbook will help develop understanding of the trait of voice. The Unit Summary provides an opportunity to practice evaluating papers for voice.

Unit Introduction: Voice

Teacher's Guide page 43
Student Traitbook page 41

Students are introduced to the unique features of voice.

Lesson 9: Help! I Need a Voice-Over!

Teacher's Guide pages 43–45
Student Traitbook pages 42–45

Students have an opportunity to rank three samples for the strength of voice, discuss results and reasons behind the ranking, and then revise one of the weaker samples to strengthen the voice.

Lesson 10: Favorite Voices

Teacher's Guide pages 46–48
Student Traitbook pages 46–49

Students hear a strong passage and discuss it, and then share favorite passages of their own in small groups. They also try imitating one favorite voice.

Lesson 11: Pumping It Up!

Teacher's Guide pages 49–51
Student Traitbook pages 50–53

Students use their analytical skills to discover those elements that contribute to voice, and then use what they have learned to transform a voiceless piece of writing.

Lesson 12: Your World, Your Voice

Teacher's Guide pages 52–54
Student Traitbook pages 54–57

Students bring all the strategies learned in previous lessons together to select a topic and create an original piece of writing with strong voice.

Unit Summary: Voice

Teacher's Guide page 55
Overhead numbers 9–12

Use the rubric on page 41 and the activities in the Summary to practice evaluating writing for strong and appropriate voice.

Teacher Rubric for Voice

6
- The writing is as individual as fingerprints.
- It begs to be read aloud—you feel a need to share it with someone.
- It is passionate, compelling, hard to put down. It explodes with energy.
- The voice is perfect for the purpose and audience.

5
- The writing is individual—probably recognizable if you know the writer.
- You would probably share this piece aloud.
- The writing shows strong feelings and is appealing to read. It has a lot of energy.
- The voice is suitable for the purpose and audience.

4
- The voice is distinctive, if not unique.
- You might share *moments* of this piece aloud.
- Snippets of passion, energy, or strong feelings are evident throughout.
- The voice is suitable for the purpose and audience but could use refining.

3
- The voice is functional and sincere, though not especially distinctive.
- The piece does not seem ready to share aloud.
- Moments of passion, energy, or strong feelings are rare.
- The voice may or may not be suitable for the purpose or audience.

2
- This voice does not stand out.
- The piece is definitely not ready to share aloud.
- The writing could use a serious energy boost. The writer sounds bored.
- The voice does not seem appropriate for the purpose or audience.

1
- The voice is difficult to find, identify, or describe.
- The piece is not one to share aloud.
- No energy or excitement comes through.
- The voice is missing or inappropriate for the purpose and audience.

Student Rubric for Voice

6
- This is *me.* It's my voice.
- I think the reader will *definitely* want to share this paper aloud with someone.
- I love my topic, and my enthusiasm and energy come through.
- The voice of this piece is perfect for my purpose.

5
- The voice sounds mostly like me.
- The reader might want to share this paper aloud.
- I like my topic, so a lot of energy comes through.
- The voice is just right for my purpose.

4
- This paper sounds like me in parts.
- The reader might share some moments here and there.
- I like my topic pretty well. The writing has *some* energy.
- The voice seems OK for my purpose.

3
- I am not sure whether this paper sounds like me or not.
- I don't think it's quite ready to share aloud yet.
- This was an OK topic, but I could not get too excited about it.
- I do not know if the voice fits my purpose.

2
- I do not think this sounds much like me.
- This paper is NOT ready to share aloud.
- I did not like my topic. I could not get excited about it.
- I don't have much voice, and I am not sure what my purpose is.

1
- I do not hear *any* voice in this writing.
- I would not share this paper aloud for anything!
- I did not like my topic one bit. It was boring.
- I do not know what my purpose for writing this is.

Recommended Books for Teaching Voice

Share a whole book, a chapter, or just a passage. As you read, do not hold back. Let the expression flow. Always ask students, *Do you hear the voice? Did this piece have more voice than that one? What voices that we have shared this week spoke to you most?*

Brooks, Bruce. 1991. *Predator!* New York: Farrar Straus Giroux. Strong nonfiction voice, great energy and detail.

Dahl, Roald. 1981. *The Twits*. New York: Puffin Books. Hilarious and unflinching voice. Great for "show me" details.

Littlechild, George. 1993. *This Land Is My Land*. San Francisco: Children's Book Press. A serious, respectful voice focusing on heritage.

Marcellino, Fred. 1999. *I, Crocodile*. New York: HarperCollins. Rollicking fun with a whimsical, unusual voice.

Paulsen, Gary. 1993. *Harris and Me*. New York: Bantam Doubleday Dell Publishing. A wild ride, combining many kinds of voices: lonely, wistful, hilarious, homesick, hopeful, fearful, and so on. In short, real life.

Polacco, Patricia. 1998. *Thank You, Mr. Falker*. New York: Philomel Books. A serious voice—but powerful.

Roberts, Willo Davis. 2001. *Buddy Is a Stupid Name for a Girl*. New York: Simon & Schuster. A reflective, personal, honest voice. Great coming of age read-aloud.

Spandel, Vicki with Ruth Nathan and Laura Robb. 2001. *The Daybook of Critical Reading and Writing* (Grade 4). Wilmington, MA: Great Source. Excellent samples of voice, fictional and nonfictional, serious to hilarious, in today's finest literature. Connects reading and writing.

More Ideas

Looking for more ideas on using literature to teach voice? We recommend *Books, Lessons, Ideas for Teaching the Six Traits: Writing in the Elementary and Middle Grades,* published by Great Source. Compiled and annotated by Vicki Spandel. For information, please phone 800-289-4490.

Help! I Need a Voice-Over!

For use with pages 42–45 in the Student Traitbook

This lesson is about hearing the voice in writing—the voice that comes through because the writer put energy into his or her work. When writers feel bored or lazy, the writing tends to drag. As listeners, we hear that, and we drag, too. Getting rid of that tired feeling is the focus here.

Objectives

Students will hear the voice—or lack of voice—in a piece of writing and have an opportunity to revise a weak piece to strengthen the voice.

Skills Focus

- Listening for voice—or lack of voice—in writing
- Connecting voice to "energy"
- Revising a piece of writing that is weak in voice
- Sharing revisions to discuss whether and how "voice-overs" work

Time Frame

Allow 30–35 minutes for this lesson.

Setting Up the Lesson

Because this lesson is about listening, you may wish to begin by sharing an excerpt from a piece of literature that has a strong voice. Ask students to listen for the voice and let you know what they hear. (See the list of recommended books on page 42 of this Teacher's Guide.)

Explain to students that when you read aloud with passion and energy, you can bring out the voice in a piece of writing. Model the difference by reading one passage in a monotone. Then reread it with expression. Ask whether students hear the difference, and encourage them to read expressively as they share writing with one another throughout this unit.

> *I don't* tell *the story to myself—I see it. I see scenes, and I write down what I see.*
>
> —Judy Blume

Teaching the Lesson

Ranking the Voice

Read aloud each sample on Student Traitbook page 43 (Shooting Hoops, Baseball Cards, and My Cousin Maria) as students follow along. Don't give the game away by the way you read a piece. Of course, when there is little or no voice present, you cannot (and should not) artificially insert it. But you can keep your voice light and pleasant even when reading "dry" writing. Give each student a few minutes to discuss and rank the three samples with a partner before discussing the items as a class.

Most students should see Sample 3 as the strongest. This is an individual voice, full of conviction, highly opinionated. It's fun to read or hear. Sample 1 is probably the second strongest. Though hardly a powerhouse in voice, it has its moments, especially the closing line: "I am a hoop-shooting machine." The writer writes as if he or she means it, though the piece lacks the individuality of Sample 3. Sample 2 is the weakest of the three. It is factual and virtually energy-free. This writer seems to be writing mostly to fill space.

Talk About the Voices

Talking about their choices helps students understand the concept. Have students share their rankings with the class.

A Voice-Lift

At the close of the discussion, invite students to select one of the weaker voices (1 or 2) to revise. Students can, of course, select Sample 3 if they truly believe they can make the voice stronger. Samples 1 and 2 are less challenging because there is much work to be done. You may wish to talk about specific ways to add voice. Remind students of the passage(s) you shared at the beginning of this lesson. They should be thinking of ways to add voice by sounding enthusiastic, adding colorful words and details, or putting more feeling into the writing.

Share and Compare

Be sure students have time to share their revisions with a partner. You may need to extend this portion into a follow-up lesson if you run out of time. Join students in their revision efforts, and share your own revision after they have had a chance to read theirs.

Extending the Lesson

- Continue to read aloud from favorite pieces with strong voice. (See page 42 of this Teacher's Guide.) Also share some pieces that are weak in voice—textbook excerpts, encyclopedias, brochures, contracts, business letters, and samples from junk mail are possibilities.

- Challenge students to find samples of writing with strong voice.

- Invite students to be readers. They should read aloud as much as possible to flex their expression "muscles" and learn to read with inflection.

Favorite Voices

For use with pages 46–49 in the Student Traitbook

In this lesson, students hear a variety of writing voices and decide which ones are most appealing. You may wish to explain that readers do not always agree on what makes a voice strong. There are many books that most readers like—books by Roald Dahl and Gary Paulsen fit into this category. But some students may select a favorite that no one else chooses, and that is fine. Writers have individual voices, and they also have individual "ears" for voice.

Objectives

Students will listen for and choose a favorite voice and then imitate it in their writing.

Skills Focus

- Listening for voice
- Identifying favorite voices
- Reading aloud with expression to share voices
- Imitating another writer's voice as a strategy for building voice

Time Frame

Because students will need time to locate their favorite books, allow two 20-minute periods for this lesson, one for each of two days. On Day 1 share the example from Susie Morgenstern. On Day 2, provide time for students to read to one another and then to write, imitating a favorite author's voice. Share the imitations as time permits.

Setting Up the Lesson

Because this lesson emphasizes identifying favorites, be ready to share some of your own favorite authors. Read aloud with plenty of expression, and remind students to do so in their writing groups when they share. Also explain why you chose each piece. It is not enough to say that a piece has voice—explain how or why you hear the voice. Does it come from detail? From passion for the topic? From a willingness to share personal feelings? Do you identify with the author's situation? As you share the reasons for your selections, you increase students' understanding of voice.

Teaching the Lesson

Sharing an Example:
Secret Letters from 0 to 10

The excerpt on Student Traitbook page 47 has several voices—the narrator, the note writers, and Victoria. Read the passage aloud, emphasizing the different voices.

What Did You Learn?

Ask students to share what they noticed about the voices in the passage.

A Voice That Stands Out

Tell students that they will have time to select their favorite books from the library, the classroom, or home. (See Student Traitbook page 47.) Some students may wish to share a passage from another source—a journal or newspaper article, for example. This is acceptable, but the voice must be one they can imitate. Encourage students to look for a striking voice, not just a pleasant one.

Share

Be sure that students rehearse before sharing their favorite passages with the group. They should read aloud to themselves—more than once if necessary—so that they can emphasize the voice.

Trying Another Voice

Imitating another's writing voice is not an easy task, so expect students to struggle a bit. In fact, this is a portion of the lesson you may wish to repeat throughout the year. Each time, students should find the task less difficult. The trick is to really listen to what the voice is like. Encourage students to discuss the voice with others in their group before writing and to find words that describe it: *irritated, shy, thoughtful, funny, blunt, timid, frightened, nervous, outgoing, friendly, happy,* and so on. It is easier to imitate a voice if you recognize the feeling the writer wants to convey.

Students will share their imitative voices in small groups, but you can also encourage volunteers to share their voices with the entire class. Then you can have some fun guessing whose voice they are imitating!

Extending the Lesson

- Repeat this lesson, asking students to choose a different voice. If the first imitation was a humorous voice, the next might be a serious voice, and so on. Share your own imitation, but do not tell students which writer you are imitating—let them guess. You can make this process simpler by giving them two or three options from which to choose. Then ask how well you did. Did you sound like the person you were trying to imitate?

- Talk about what happens when you use someone else's voice. Do you lose part of your own voice? Or does the other person's voice become a little part of you? Do you think that little part will fade over time?

- Encourage students to continue reading their writing aloud. It is difficult to hear or increase voice in your own writing if you do not hear it read aloud with expression.

- Make a list of favorite voices. Of all the voices you and your students have read and heard during this lesson, which are your favorites? Use your choices to make a poster to keep on the wall as a reminder.

Pumping It Up!

For use with pages 50–53 in the Student Traitbook

This lesson invites students to become more analytical. They have listened for, selected, and imitated favorite voices. Now it's time to begin thinking about which elements in a piece of writing really contribute to voice. What can we simply not do without if we want writing to have voice?

Objectives

Students will increase their understanding of voice by comparing two writing samples: one rich with voice, one virtually voiceless. As students compare, they should see how details and feelings contribute to voice. Finally, they will use what they have learned through this comparison to revise a piece that is weak in voice.

Skills Focus

- Listening for voice in a passage
- Recognizing the elements that help create or shape voice in a piece of writing
- Comparing two versions of the same passage to see how omitting detail and feeling affects voice
- Expressing personal reactions to two very different pieces of writing
- Revising a piece weak in voice by adding details and feelings

Time Frame

Allow 40 minutes for this lesson. You can divide it into two 20-minute lessons by saving the writing activity called "Pumping Up the Voice" (the revision) for the second lesson.

Setting Up the Lesson

Bring in a deflated balloon and blow it up to dramatize "pumping it up." Talk about how everything changes as you inflate an object: size, shape, color, and so on. Model one or two simple, one-line passages on the overhead for students: *Fred was frightened.* (Deflated) *Fred's knees turned to jelly when the 100-pound ball of snarling fur leaped over the porch rail at his chest.* (Pumped up.) Another way to do this is to have students give you the simple sentences first. Then you can add the details and feelings. After working on three or four of these examples, give students a simple sentence and see what they can do with it. This is a great warm-up to the longer revision they will do later in the lesson.

Teaching the Lesson

Sharing an Example:
The Sign of the Beaver

The passage on Traitbook page 51 rings with voice, but it's a quiet voice. You may wish to prepare students for this before they read—or you can let them pick up on it for themselves. Use your judgment. Sometimes the quiet voices are a little tougher to hear, but they're very important. As we listen to voices like those in the Elizabeth Speare piece, we teach ourselves to "tune in" to different kinds of voices—a good thing because every voice is unique.

What Did You See? *What Did You* Feel?

Encourage students to record the strongest images and feelings in the samples on Student Traitbook page 52. The main point is that images and feelings abound in Sample 1, but hardly exist in Sample 2—unless you add them from your own imagination. Help students connect images and feelings to the trait of voice. Explain that by adding detail and sharing feelings, you can make the voice in any piece stronger. Comparing Sample 1 to Sample 2 shows this to be true.

Where Does Voice Come From?

Invite students to share, as a class, some of the images and feelings they recorded from Sample 1. Talk about how these contributed to the voice. Then talk about the lack of these items in Sample 2. Does this writing have *any* voice?

Pumping Up the Voice

Encourage students to really "let go" with their revisions of "The Best Day of Summer." They should have fun, adding mountains of details and putting in plenty of feelings. This story has lots of potential. River rafting should be a wild adventure, but this writer sounds no more excited than if she or he were describing how to make a sandwich. Remind students that *telling* is not *showing,* and that only showing leads to voice. The writer says that he or she "was really excited." But what does excitement look like? How does your face look? How do you act? How does your stomach feel? Saying "I was really excited" is not a detail. "I bit my lip to keep from yelling as we hurled over the rapids, and gasped as water flooded my face. I couldn't see or breathe and my stomach was one huge knot—but I didn't want to stop!" Now *that* has voice!

Share and Compare

Have partners share and compare how they added voice to the passage. Encourage acceptance of different ways to revise voice.

Extending the Lesson

- Share revisions of "The Best Day of Summer" aloud. Talk about any new details or feelings you hear in the revisions and how they contribute to the voice.

- Discuss the differences between boisterous or humorous voices and quieter, more philosophical voices. Do students have a preference? Does one kind of voice speak to them more?

- What are some words students would use to describe their own voices at this time? Make a class poster and add the words as students suggest them. Do not forget to contribute your own.

- Play music. Try a few very different selections—perhaps contemporary, country-western, classical, and so on—and ask students to describe these musical voices. What do they feel as they listen? What kinds of voices do they hear? Why does one voice appeal to listeners while another doesn't? Can a piece of music have voice just the way a piece of writing does? Have students write about this.

Your World, Your Voice

For use with pages 54–57 in the Student Traitbook

This lesson is a celebration of individuality. Who you are has a lot to do with how your voice sounds. You might begin by telling students a few things about yourself that they do not know, such as a scary experience you had, a time you got lost, something you're good at that has nothing to do with your life in school, or a favorite car or pet. It could be anything at all! Encourage your students to consider what makes them individuals.

Objectives

Students will bring together all the previous strategies they have learned: imitating a strong voice, using detail, keeping the energy level high, and sharing feelings.

Skills Focus

- Thinking about personally important topics
- Choosing a personally important topic about which to write
- Creating a piece of writing with strong voice
- Coming up with language to describe one's personal voice
- Assessing a piece of personal writing for voice

Time Frame

Allow 30–35 minutes for this lesson.

Setting Up the Lesson

If it is available, read aloud Byrd Baylor's *I'm in Charge of Celebrations*, a book that celebrates seeing the world in your own way, through your own eyes. The book's narrator celebrates little things, such as seeing a double rainbow, seeing a wild rabbit or coyote, and so on. If you do not have the book, talk about seeing the world in your own way. Talk about how little things are worth celebrating because they tell us who we are. You may wish to brainstorm a list of personal celebrations: finding a special rock, hearing your favorite song on the radio, making a friend, eating something you haven't tasted before, discovering a new "special place," and so on.

Also spend some time talking about personally important topics. Make a list of things you like to write about and explain why. Keep your list fairly short—four or five topics are plenty. Ask students to make personal lists and to share them in response groups. Encourage borrowing; if one student thinks of a topic another would like to write about, encourage that student to add the topic to his or her list. When students write, they can choose from this list or from the list under "Setting Your Voice Free." The important thing is for students to choose topics about which they have strong feelings.

Teaching the Lesson

Setting Your Voice Free

On Student Traitbook page 55, students will choose a writing topic. Students should have two lists from which to select a topic: the one in the Traitbook and the one you brainstormed together. Still, they should feel free to add a new topic if they think of something else.

A Little Help

Are your students familiar with prewriting, or is this technique new to them? Their experience will make a big difference on how much time you spend on this portion of the lesson. If students are not familiar with how to make an idea web, create a word collection, or list questions, model these techniques for them, or model at least two prewriting strategies you know and use. Then encourage them to take time for this important part of writing. Prewriting stimulates thinking and usually leads to much stronger voice.

Writing

When students have finished some prewriting, give them time to work on their drafts. They should have at least 12 minutes of uninterrupted writing time. Stretch it to 15 or 20 minutes if their attention spans permit. During this time, you can move around the room answering questions and offering suggestions to students who are having difficulty. Refer them to two sources of inspiration: (1) sensory details—How did it look, sound, feel, smell, or taste? and (2) personal feelings—How did you feel about what happened? Encourage students to let their feelings come through in their writing.

Pause and Reflect

This lesson allows for some personal reflection, and you may want to walk students through it step-by-step. First (after noting the topic or title), students are asked to come up with words to describe their own voice. This is challenging, so you may wish to list some possibilities on the overhead or chalkboard: *funny, angry, sad, lazy, frantic, worried, joyful, excited, wild and crazy,* and so on.

Rating Your Voice

Next, students are asked to rate themselves on voice. Remind them to be honest. If voice is not there, they should honestly record that, and think about ways to make it stronger. But if the voice is powerful, they should mark this accordingly.

Extending the Lesson

- With students, rate other pieces of writing for voice and discuss what gives the stronger pieces their power.

- With the students, make a list of things that contribute to voice; turn the list into a poster called "Tips for Strong Voice." Hang the poster in your classroom.

- Friendly letters tend to have voice because the audience is built in. You know who it is you are writing to. Write some letters individually or as a class. You might write to local business people (asking for information or praising something done well), to sports figures, celebrities, musicians, or favorite authors. Read some of the letters aloud and make a class book with letters and responses. Which responses have the most voice? Why?

Voice

Teacher's Guide pages 41, 142–154
Overhead numbers 9–12

Objectives

Students will review and apply what they have learned about the trait of voice.

Reviewing Voice

Review with students what they have learned about the trait of voice. Ask students to discuss what voice means and to explain why it is important in a piece of writing. Then ask them to recall the main points about voice that are discussed in Unit 3. Students' responses should include the following points:

- Look for voice in others' writing.
- Make your readers see and feel what is happening.
- Develop your own voice.

Applying Voice

To help students apply what they have learned about voice, distribute copies of the Student Rubric for Voice on page 41 of this Teacher's Guide. Students will use these to score one or more sample papers that can be found beginning on page 115. The papers for voice are also on overhead transparencies 9–12.

Before students score the papers, explain that a rubric is a grading system to determine the score a piece of writing should receive for a particular trait. Preview the Student Rubric for Voice, pointing out that a paper very strong in voice receives a score of 6, and a paper very weak in voice receives a score of 1. Tell students to read the rubric and then to read the paper to be scored. Then tell them to look at the paper and the rubric together to determine the score the paper should receive. Encourage students to make notes on each paper to help them score it. For example, they might put a check mark next to sentences in which a strong voice emerges.

Overview

In this unit, students will think about the "choice" part of word choice. Student writers understand that good writers make choices based on specific strategies: using verbs to give writing energy, for instance, or using sensory words to create vivid pictures and impressions.

The focus of the instruction in this unit will be
- increasing students' awareness of the power of verbs in their writing.
- giving students practice in extracting word meaning from context so that they are continually adding new words to their vocabularies.
- encouraging students to enrich their writing with sensory detail.
- showing students how to cut "clutter" from over-inflated writing.

Word Choice: *A Definition*

Word choice refers to the language a writer chooses to express his or her ideas. Effective words are both clear and colorful. The more precise the word, the clearer the meaning. *Tree* is not as precise, for instance, as *redwood*. Add a few descriptive words and strong verbs, and we get a vivid word picture: *Towering redwoods continued their seemingly endless climb into forever, and I wished myself a hawk, perched on the tip of this giant's fingers, viewing the world from such a noble height.* As with any trait, appropriate word choice depends on audience and purpose. In a business letter, writing must be crisp, clean, and to the point. In a poem, the writer can be a little more playful, using words in unexpected ways.

The Unit at a Glance

The following lessons in the Teacher's Guide and practice exercises in the Student Traitbook will help develop understanding of the trait of word choice. The Unit Summary provides an opportunity to practice evaluating papers for word choice.

Unit Introduction: Word Choice

Teacher's Guide page 61
Student Traitbook page 58

Students are introduced to the unique features of word choice.

Lesson 13: Verbs of Steel

Teacher's Guide pages 61–63
Student Traitbook pages 59–62

Students have an opportunity to recognize strong verbs and to create original text using the strongest verbs they can muster.

Lesson 14: Using Context

Teacher's Guide pages 64–66
Student Traitbook pages 63–66

Students learn the meaning of "context" and how to use context clues in making educated guesses about the meaning of a new word.

Lesson 15: Painting Word Pictures

Teacher's Guide pages 67–69
Student Traitbook pages 67–70

Students experiment with the use of sensory language, first in the writing of others, and then in their own writing.

Lesson 16: Pop That Balloon—Revise to Clarify

Teacher's Guide pages 70–72
Student Traitbook pages 71–74

Students learn to get rid of overblown words and phrases, simplifying and clarifying through revision.

Unit Summary: Word Choice

Teacher's Guide page 73
Overhead numbers 13–16

Use the rubric on page 59 and the activities in the Summary to practice evaluating writing for word choice.

Teacher Rubric for Word Choice

6
- The writing is clear, striking, original, and precise.
- The writer uses powerful verbs to energize the writing.
- Sensory language, as appropriate, greatly enhances meaning.
- The writing is concise; each word counts.

5
- The writing is clear and often original.
- The writer relies more on strong verbs than on modifiers to enrich meaning.
- Sensory language, as appropriate, adds detail.
- The writing is reasonably concise; a word or phrase here and there could be cut.

4
- The writing is clear in most cases. Some words or phrases are vague or confusing.
- The writer uses some strong verbs and may rely too heavily on modifiers.
- Sensory language is present.
- Writing is usually concise; some wordiness appears.

3
- The writing is often unclear, misleading, or vague, though the main idea comes through.
- The reader needs to use strong verbs. Modifiers are overused.
- Sensory language is minimal or is overused.
- The writing may be short but is not necessarily concise. Some clutter is evident.

2
- Many words and phrases are misused, vague, or unclear. The writer's main message is not clear.
- Strong verbs are rare or missing.
- Sensory language is minimal or absent.
- Word use may be skimpy or cluttered; either way, meaning is hard to determine.

1
- Words and phrases are vague, confusing, or simply misused.
- Verbs are weak throughout; the writing lacks energy.
- Sensory language is missing.
- Word choice seems random. Words create no clear meaning.

Student Rubric for Word Choice

6
- Every word helps make my meaning clear.
- My verbs are powerful and lively. They give my writing energy!
- My words paint a clear picture in the reader's mind.
- I got rid of any clutter.

5
- My words are clear most of the time.
- I used a lot of strong verbs.
- My words paint a picture. Readers can tell what I'm trying to say.
- I got rid of most clutter. I don't think it's a problem.

4
- My words are clear most of the time. I think readers can figure out my main idea.
- I used some strong verbs, but I could use more.
- Some of my words paint a picture. Some are vague.
- My writing has *some* clutter. I have a few unnecessary words.

3
- My word choice is unclear in many places. Readers might not guess my main idea.
- I think I have *some* strong verbs.
- Readers might be able to picture what I am talking about.
- My writing is cluttered. I used too many unnecessary words.

2
- My words are not very clear. It is hard to tell what I am saying.
- I do not know for sure whether I used verbs. I am not sure what a verb is.
- It is hard to picture what I am talking about.
- I do not know for sure whether I used too many words or not enough words. I just wrote.

1
- My words are hard to understand. I am not sure what I want to say.
- I do not know whether I used verbs. What is a verb?
- I don't think readers can picture what I am talking about yet.
- Maybe I used too many words. Maybe I used the wrong words. I don't know.

Recommended Books
for Teaching Word Choice

As you share literature—strong or weak in word choice—remember to ask your students questions like these: *Which words did you like? Did you hear any new words you could add to your personal dictionary? Did you hear words that were unclear or overused? Did you notice any verbs or sensory words that added power or detail to the writing?*

Fleischman, Paul. 1999. *Weslandia.* New York: Scholastic, Inc. Wonderful for extracting meaning from context.

Florian, Douglas. 1998. *Insectlopedia.* New York: Harcourt Brace & Company. A festival of word play. Shows how to have fun with language. Also good for strong verbs.

Fox, Mem. 1996. *Feathers and Fools.* New York: Harcourt Brace. Strong verbs, good for extracting meaning from context.

Laden, Nina. 2000. *Roberto the Insect Architect.* San Francisco: Chronicle Books. Excellent for strong verbs and unusual modifiers.

Johnston, Tony. 1998. *Bigfoot Cinderrrrella.* New York: G. P. Putnam's Sons. Excellent for strong verbs.

Paulsen, Gary. 1999. *Canoe Days.* New York: Bantam Doubleday Dell. Shows the beauty of concise, simple language used well.

Steig, William. 1986. *Brave Irene.* New York: Farrar, Straus and Giroux. Strong verbs, concise writing, excellent sensory detail.

More Ideas

Looking for more ideas on using literature to teach word choice? We recommend *Books, Lessons, Ideas for Teaching the Six Traits: Writing in the Elementary and Middle Grades,* published by Great Source. Compiled and annotated by Vicki Spandel. This book is thoughtfully annotated and contains many lesson ideas. For information, please phone 800-289-4490.

Verbs of steel

For use with pages 59–62 in the Student Traitbook

This lesson emphasizes the importance of *verbs* to give writing energy. Also, because verbs are action words, they enhance imagery. While all words are important, verbs are more powerful than, say, adjectives—which students often use to add detail. One good verb can usually upstage a whole cast of adjectives. Compare "The lion felt *hungry*" (adjective) to "The lion *crouched* low in the brush, *stalking* the zebra—who *noticed* nothing" (verbs).

Objectives

Students will become aware of strong verbs, practice comparing strong and weak verbs, and create original text using strong verbs.

Skills Focus

- Listening and reading for strong verbs
- Comparing two passages: one with weak verbs, one with strong verbs
- Discussing the power of verbs in writing
- Creating a piece of original writing using strong verbs

Time Frame

Allow 40 minutes for this lesson, excluding Extending the Lesson activities. You may divide the lesson by saving the writing activity for a separate lesson. You will then have two 20-minute lessons.

Setting Up the Lesson

This lesson depends heavily on students' understanding of what a **verb** is, so spend some time discussing verbs. Explain that verbs are action words. They describe what we do or what other things in the world do. Give a few examples: *dash, tease, march, hiss, hiccup, collide, embrace.* Now, make two lists: **Verbs** and **Other Words.** Give students a random list of words: *jump, swing, float, marsh, frog, joy, laugh.* Let them tell you in which list to put each word. Some words will fit on both lists: I had to **laugh** (verb) or Jill had an unforgettable **laugh** (noun). You can make the difference clear by using the word in a sentence. Then ask, "Is this an action word?"

Verbs energize writing in a way that other words cannot. Although precise nouns and adjectives are effective, nothing replaces a powerful verb for sheer force; using verbs relates to the idea of "showing" rather than "telling." You can demonstrate this idea by revising a simple sentence containing an adjective. Turn the sentence into one with a strong verb that brings out the meaning of the sentence. Do this on the overhead. Here are some examples:

It was **hot.** (adjective)

Jack **mopped** his forehead and **gulped** down his third glass of water. (verbs)

Betty seemed **upset** about dinner. (adjective)

Betty **shrieked** when she thought she saw the spaghetti **wriggle.** (verbs)

After doing three or four of these, you might ask your students to help you revise the following sentences: The car was **messy.** Running up the hill was **hard.** The movie was **boring.**

Teaching the Lesson

Sharing an Example: The BFG
Read aloud the excerpt on Student Traitbook page 60, asking students to follow along. Emphasize the verbs. They already appear in boldface, and you may wish to remind students of this so that they can easily spot the verbs as they read.

After sharing the passage, ask students how the verbs helped create images in their minds. Did they have favorites? Also ask whether there are any verbs they did not understand (you might quiz them to be sure). Explain the meaning of any new verbs. Are there any verbs they'd like to borrow to use in their own writing? This is a good time to introduce the concept of a personal dictionary: a place for storing new, favorite words. A personal dictionary is handier than a regular dictionary because it is in the students' notebooks and contains words they picked themselves.

Goodbye, Strong Verbs

The directions ask students to read the revised excerpt from *The BFG* on their own, but you may wish to read it aloud to help emphasize the differences in verbs. Remind students that the boldfaced words in this piece replace the boldfaced words in the original. It's the same story—only the verbs have been changed.

Your Response

Make sure that students verbalize their comparisons between the two pieces and fill out the "Your Response" section. Check to see how many students liked the first version better. Be sure to ask them why.

Finding Verbs of Steel

The portion of the lesson on Student Traitbook page 61 reinforces what students have learned by making them spot the verbs in a passage with no boldfaced clues. They should find many strong verbs in this passage: *flipped, slanted, creaked, prayed, hold together, scraping, scrounging,* and so on. If they do not, have them read again, or you may wish to review the definition of a verb to make the search easier. Be sure students do the underlining on their own first.

Share and Compare

Have student partners compare their work. This is important because otherwise some students will let the partner do all the choosing.

Your Own Steel

Because this writing lesson focuses on using verbs, suggest that students choose a topic that is full of action. A good prewriting activity is to generate a verb list as students picture themselves in action. For example, if a student chose "A Family Outing" as his or her topic, the verb list might include *driving, suffocating* (in the back seat), *singing, starving, swimming,* and *cooling down* (in the water). After students finish their writing, have them share in response groups or ask volunteers to share their writing with the entire class.

Extending the Lesson

- Keep a running list of "Favorite Verbs" posted on the wall, and add to it each time students come up with a good entry. Students can also add favorite verbs to their personal dictionaries.
- Continue to read aloud from pieces that have strong verbs.
- Notice when students use strong verbs in their writing. Comment on this, letting them know how the verbs helped you picture the action.

Using Context

For use with pages 63–66 in the Student Traitbook

Word choice implies that student writers have a cache of words from which to choose. One way to develop this personal storehouse is through reading. Avid readers continually pick up new vocabulary words. But doing this requires a little reader's trick: figuring out meaning from *context.* To define a word, readers must use the clues a writer provides within a sentence or paragraph. Good readers may not even be conscious of it, but they routinely think to themselves, "This word *probably* means . . ." How do they know? Because of context—how the word is used.

Objectives

Students will understand how to use context—the way a word is used in a sentence—to determine meaning. They will recognize the importance of adding new words to their personal word caches regularly.

Skills Focus

- Understanding the concept of *context*
- Guessing at word meanings out of context
- Guessing at word meanings using context

Time Frame

Allow 30 minutes for this lesson, excluding Extending the Lesson.

Setting Up the Lesson

Students need to understand that seeing a word in context means seeing how it is used in a sentence (or sometimes, in a paragraph).

Author William Steig is good at making word meaning clear from context. His children's books are renowned for their use of "adult vocabulary," but teachers and readers of all ages acknowledge that although Steig uses many sophisticated words, the way in which he uses them usually makes the meaning quite clear. You might, therefore, start this lesson by sharing all or part of one of Steig's books, giving students just a few words to listen for and guess at before you read. Remember, they'll have much more practice with this shortly, so keep this warm-up simple. Also, feel free to use any book by any author. (Some books by William Steig: *Amos and Boris, Brave Irene, Sylvester and the Magic Pebble, The Amazing Bone, Dr. DeSoto*)

Teaching the Lesson

Words out of Context

On Student Traitbook page 64, students discover how difficult it is to determine the meaning of a word that is not used in a sentence. That is what *out of context* means. Tell students that this is not a test—it's a guessing game. They should make any guesses at the word meanings that they can. Reassure them that they will have another chance later because they are going to see these words again—but then the words will be used in context (in sentences). They might try to recall whether they have heard the word before or decide whether it reminds them of another word. They should make their guesses quickly and move on.

Putting Words Back in Context

Once again, students are challenged to determine word meanings but this time they have context to help them. Having a sentence or paragraph to go by makes the guessing game much easier, even when the word is new and difficult. Again, encourage students to make guesses. If they get stuck, tell them to read the piece again. As an alternative, you may wish to read the piece aloud after the students have read it on their own.

Be ready to point out clues. Take *delectable,* for example. We know it's part of the "perfect diet." What might that mean? Perfect sounds pretty good, so delectable food is probably—what? Nauseating? Never. Repulsive? No way. Delicious? That sounds right. If you help students work through one clue, it is easier for them to understand how the "in context" clue process works.

Discuss and Check

Be sure to go over all word meanings after students have finished guessing. Allow for some variety; there is more than one way to define each word. Sometimes, too, it's hard to verbalize the definition of a new word. Help students by asking them to describe what the crocodile is doing or feeling. What's his attitude? What expression does he have on his face? Just because you cannot come up with the perfect synonym is not a sign you do not have a general idea about what a word means.

Extending the Lesson

- Continue the "in context" practice when you encounter other words that students do not know. Instead of simply giving them a definition, write a line or two on the overhead and ask them to guess. With enough practice, this guessing becomes a habit.

- When you use a word that students do not recognize, encourage them to ask you to "put it in context," or use it in a sentence. Do so, and see whether they can determine the meaning from the way you use the word. Good writers learn to use context to make meaning clear.

- Encourage students to collect interesting words from their everyday reading and listening.

- Play the guessing game with one word each day, choosing a word students need to know for their current studies. Let them guess "out of context" first; then, put the word in context. If they still cannot define it, use the word in another sentence. Continue until students can state at least a partial definition.

Painting Word Pictures

For use with pages 67–70 in the Student Traitbook

Sensory language makes writing vivid. It helps readers see, hear, smell, taste, and touch every experience the writer describes. *The scent of warm cinnamon bread wafted out the window and beckoned to Sara* is much more powerful than *The bread smelled good.* When students learn the power of sensory language, they can put any experience within the reader's grasp.

Objectives

Students will understand the meaning of sensory language, identify such language, and use sensory language in their own writing.

Skills Focus

- Learning the meaning of the term *sensory language*
- Identifying sensory details in a piece of writing
- Creating a sensory detail table as a form of prewriting
- Creating a piece of writing that includes sensory details

Time Frame

Allow 40 minutes for this lesson. You can divide it into two 20-minute lessons by saving the part called "Your Turn to Write!" for the second lesson.

Setting Up the Lesson

Explain to students that **sensory details** are any details that appeal to the five senses: seeing, hearing, smelling, tasting, and touching.

Ask students to imagine themselves, as a class, in one place (you choose), perhaps at a theater, in a cave, on the beach, in a city, or at the rodeo. Then ask them to list all the sights they can think of, then the sounds, the smells, and so on. Go through the senses systematically—you want students to think of as many examples of each sense as they can. Expect students to notice different things. That's OK. You're creating a kind of collage of impressions. List their thoughts on the overhead. Then, ask whether they think they could write a description of this place that would include ALL of these details.

> *Never use a long word where a short one will do.*
>
> —George Orwell

Teaching the Lesson

Sharing an Example: Mud Fights

Ask students whether they have ever had a mud fight. What do they recall? Then, read Jocelyn's poem (Student Traitbook pages 67–68) aloud slowly so that students can take in as many details as possible. Suggest that they close their eyes as you read to tune out any distractions. Ask them to imagine that they are right there, part of the mud fight. Now what do they *see, hear, touch, taste,* or *smell?* Here's a question to think about: Do readers sometimes add sensory details from their own experiences, even if the writer doesn't mention them? Is this a good thing or not?

Sensory Reaction

Students have already underlined sensory details from Jocelyn's poem. Now they can compare what they noticed with the details shown in the table. This portion of the lesson helps students see how to organize sensory details, much as you did with the warm-up when you introduced the lesson. They do NOT need to agree with everything. Perhaps they noticed or thought of other details that are not mentioned directly in the poem. Encourage them to expand the list as they compare. Also, if they missed something completely, help them find the reference in the poem.

Making Your Own Chart

The part of the lesson on Student Traitbook page 69 expands what students have just learned by asking them to list all the details they notice as readers. This text is rich with sensory detail, but it is not essential to use every column or to notice everything. Each student should easily find five or six details to list. Some will find many more. Be sure to ask whether the writer could have used different words or additional details to make the nasty chore of garage cleaning even more vivid.

Your Turn to Write!

This part of the lesson begins with a strong **prewriting** activity: listing sensory details. Use the term *prewriting,* and let students know that it is a good strategy when you are writing a description. Make your own list on an overhead transparency, but do not show it to students until their lists are finished. You do not want them to copy your list.

Be sure that students choose only one of the topics: a time you had to do a chore you did not like or a time you had fun with a friend. Then they should decide whether to write a poem or a paragraph. Because a poem is often made up of phrases, the list of details takes a poetry writer about halfway home. You may wish to keep this in mind when advising your writers. The paragraph is a little more challenging.

Remind poetry writers that poems do not have to rhyme. You want them searching for the right word—not the rhyming word.

Share

Be sure to give students opportunities to share their writing in response groups or with the class as a whole. Share yours as well. Explain how you used your prewriting list of details as the basis for your draft. If you omitted some details or added more, point this out. Prewriting is meant to get you started. It should not put you in a box so that you can write only what's on your list.

Extending the Lesson

- Share pieces of literature in which sensory details are strong, and ask students to tell you which ones they remember best. (See the list of recommended books on page 60 of this Teacher's Guide.) Make a list.

- With your students, generate a list of potential writing topics that lend themselves to the use of sensory detail.

- Ask each student to write on one of the topics from your list (or to come up with another). You write, too. Have students share their sensory detail papers and add them to their writing folders.

Pop That Balloon— Revise to Clarify

For use with pages 71–74 in the Student Traitbook

This lesson focuses on getting rid of inflated language. This task is one of the most difficult things a writer must do. We all "fall in love" with our own writing. It's only natural. It's important for students to realize, however, that as wonderful as descriptive words are, they can be overused.

Objectives

Students will understand that inflated language is hard to understand and that a concise, simple way of expressing ideas is often the clearest and most appealing.

Skills Focus

- Understanding the concept of "big balloon," or overblown, writing
- Assessing a piece of writing for wordiness
- Revising a wordy piece to make it more concise
- Evaluating personal skill in making wordy writing more concise

Time Frame

Allow about 35 minutes for this lesson, excluding Extending the Lesson. The portion of the lesson called "Revising to Clarify" can be saved for a separate lesson.

Setting Up the Lesson

When does enough turn into too much? That's really the underlying question of this lesson. Writers who hold back on necessary words make it hard for readers to understand what they are talking about. But it is also possible to overdo it. You can illustrate this in a number of ways; for example, blow up a balloon and ask students to tell you when it reaches the "just right" point. Naturally, some students will want you to go as far as possible till the balloon bursts, and this is a good illustration of the "too much" principle. You might also consider sketching an aquarium—when does it have enough fish? Are 5 enough? 10? How about 20? Keep adding fish till your students say "Enough!" For another example, ask students to bring in three extra layers of clothes, and have them put all of them on in your class. Ask students how it feels to wear all that clothing. They will probably say that it is uncomfortable.

Teaching the Lesson

Sharing an Example: A Forest Full of Trees, Animals, Other Living Creatures, and a Trail

The sample on Student Traitbook page 72 is very wordy. How many times can you use the word *winding* in one paragraph? Some students may like it, though; student writers sometimes subscribe to "the more description, the better" theory.

Your Response

Have students discuss their reactions to the piece. Most will find it extremely wordy. Emphasize that wordy writing is unappealing because reading it is such hard work. To make the point, ask one of your students to read the piece aloud.

Checking Out Our Revision

Students have now had a chance to revise the wordy paragraph by crossing out unnecessary words. Probably, most students did not cut quite as much as we did. This is normal for beginning writers of any age. Their revision need not match that in the text. What is important is that they found some parts to cut.

Share and Compare

Remind student writers that cutting words or phrases is a good idea as long as meaning is not lost. Explain, too, that each writer will revise a bit differently. The sample has many redundant passages: *The Nature Park is a gorgeous beautifully forested area with a trail winding back and forth through it like a snake winding back and forth through the green grass.* You can cut many words without losing meaning: *The Nature Park is a beautiful forested area with a trail that winds through it like a snake.* Note the difference: 18 words instead of 29.

Revising to Clarify: The "Big" City

This time, encourage students to be a little bolder with their red pens and cut anything that is not needed for meaning. Make the paragraph short and snappy. Here's a hint: If students have not chopped off at least 20 words, they have not cut enough. Ask them to try again. Brave revisers will cut this paragraph in half.

Share and Compare

Revise with students on an overhead transparency, and show them your revision when you finish. Ask student partners to compare their revisions with each other and then with yours.

Extending the Lesson

- Write a draft on any topic and deliberately make it wordy. Let students see the original on the overhead. Read it aloud, and have them rate it: very wordy, a little wordy, or not wordy. Comment on their ratings, and ask their advice in cutting to improve it.

- Ask each student to create a wordy piece for his or her partner to revise. Tell them to put in as many unnecessary words as they can. Students should trade papers for the revising part of the lesson, popping those over-inflated balloons. Post the "before" and "after" examples for student reference.

Word Choice

Teacher's Guide pages 59, 155–167
Overhead numbers 13–16

Objectives

Students will review and apply what they have learned about the trait of word choice.

Reviewing Word Choice

Review with students what they have learned about the trait of word choice. Ask students to discuss what word choice means and to explain why it is important in a piece of writing. Then ask them to recall the main points about word choice that are discussed in Unit 4. Students' responses should include the following points:

- Choose verbs that give your writing energy.
- Learn new words to enliven your writing.
- Describe with sensory words.
- Delete unnecessary words.

Applying Word Choice

To help students apply what they have learned about word choice, distribute copies of the Student Rubric for Word Choice on page 59 of this Teacher's Guide. Students will use these to score one or more sample papers that can be found beginning on page 115. The papers for word choice are also on overhead transparencies 13–16.

Before students score the papers, explain that a rubric is a grading system to determine the score a piece of writing should receive for a particular trait. Preview the Student Rubric for Word Choice, pointing out that a paper very strong in word choice receives a score of 6, and a paper very weak in word choice receives a score of 1. Tell students to read the rubric and then to read the paper to be scored. Then tell them to look at the paper and the rubric together to determine the score the paper should receive. Encourage students to make notes on each paper to help them score it. For example, they might underline particularly strong verbs or descriptive language and draw a line through unnecessary words.

Overview

Sentence fluency is about the flow and rhythm of writing—how it plays to the ear, not just to the eye. Fluent writing has cadence and a smooth, lyrical, quality. One sentence flows into another, and the piece invites expressive oral reading.

The focus of the instruction in this unit will be

- showing students how to vary sentence beginnings.
- making students aware of run-on sentences and how to fix them.
- ensuring that students read their writing aloud to determine whether it sounds natural.
- providing many opportunities for students to practice revising text that has problems with sentence fluency.

Sentence Fluency: *A Definition*

Sentence fluency is the rhythm and flow of language, especially as that rhythm and flow enhance clarity. Passages strong in fluency are marked by a smooth cadence, noticeable variety in sentence length and structure, readily identifiable connections between sentences, and an absence of such problems as choppiness or run-ons. Fluent writing is a pleasure to read aloud. In fact, fluency is a trait more often noticeable to the ear than to the eye.

Sentence fluency and sentence structure are not the same. Although grammar sometimes plays a role in achieving fluency, this unit focuses more on sentence variety and readability than on grammatical correctness.

The Unit at a Glance

The following lessons in the Teacher's Guide and practice exercises in the Student Traitbook will help develop understanding of the trait of sentence fluency. The Unit Summary provides an opportunity to practice evaluating papers for sentence fluency.

Unit Introduction: Sentence Fluency

Teacher's Guide page 79
Student Traitbook page 75

Students are introduced to the unique features of sentence fluency.

Lesson 17: Spice Up Your Sentences

Teacher's Guide pages 79–81
Student Traitbook pages 76–79

Students assess text for variety and revise a weak sample to increase fluency by altering sentence beginnings.

Lesson 18: Just Say No to Run-ons

Teacher's Guide pages 82–84
Student Traitbook pages 80–83

Students learn two strategies for identifying and resolving common run-on problems.

Lesson 19: Authentic Conversation

Teacher's Guide pages 85–87
Student Traitbook pages 84–87

Students assess a sample of dialogue and then revise another sample to give it the sound of real people speaking.

Lesson 20: Read and Rank

Teacher's Guide pages 88–90
Student Traitbook pages 88–91

Students use what they have learned in the first three lessons to rank three pieces of text for fluency. Following this warm-up, they use listening skills to assess and revise a piece that is weak in fluency, and then compare their revisions to the author's polished original.

Unit Summary: Sentence Fluency

Teacher's Guide page 91
Overhead numbers 17–20

Use the rubric on page 77 and the activities in the Summary to practice evaluating writing for sentence fluency.

Teacher Rubric for Sentence Fluency

6
- The writing is smooth, natural, and easy to read.
- Virtually every sentence begins differently, adding interest to the text.
- Dialogue, if used, sounds natural and conversational.
- The piece invites expressive oral reading that brings out the voice.

5
- The writing is smooth and easy to read.
- Many sentences begin differently.
- Dialogue, if used, sounds natural.
- The piece is a pleasure to read aloud.

4
- The writing is easy to read in most places. There may be a few choppy sentences.
- Some sentences begin differently; there is also a little repetition.
- Dialogue, if used, sounds reasonably natural, though a little stiff in spots.
- With some rehearsal, their piece can be read aloud easily.

3
- The writing is sometimes easy to read. Choppy sentences, run-ons, or other problems may necessitate some rereading.
- Sentence beginnings tend to be alike.
- Dialogue, if used, does not sound like actual speech.
- Rehearsal is needed before reading this piece aloud.

2
- The writing is often difficult to follow. Choppy sentences, run-ons, or other problems require continual rereading.
- Many sentences begin the same way.
- Dialogue, if used, does not sound natural or conversational.
- The piece is hard to read aloud, even with rehearsal.

1
- The writing is consistently difficult to follow. Choppiness, run-ons, or other sentence problems abound.
- Sentences consistently begin with the same word or phrase, or it is hard to tell *where* they begin.
- Dialogue, if used, is hard to follow.
- The piece is difficult to read aloud, even with rehearsal.

Student Rubric for Sentence Fluency

6
- My writing is clear, smooth, and easy to read. It flows!
- Sentences begin in *many* different ways.
- If I used dialogue, it sounds great. It sounds like real people talking.
- Readers will love reading this paper aloud with lots of expression.

5
- My writing is clear and smooth most of the time. I think it's pretty easy to read.
- Most of my sentences begin in different ways.
- If I used dialogue, I did a good job. It sounds real to me.
- I think readers will like reading this paper aloud. It sounds smooth.

4
- Some of my writing is smooth. It needs work here and there.
- Some sentences begin in different ways. A lot begin the same way, though.
- If I used dialogue, I did fine. It sounds like real people talking.
- Reading this paper aloud takes a little work.

3
- A lot of my writing needs smoothing out. I might have choppy sentences or run-ons.
- A few sentences begin in different ways. A lot of my beginnings are the same.
- If I used dialogue, it needs work. It doesn't sound like real people talking.
- It is not easy to read this paper aloud, but it can be done.

2
- My writing is bumpy! I have choppy sentences, run-ons, or other problems.
- I did not worry about sentence beginnings. Many of them are the same.
- I do not think my dialogue sounds like real people talking.
- It is hard to read this paper aloud. I tried and it was even hard for me.

1
- My writing is very hard to read. I can't tell one sentence from another.
- It is hard to tell where my sentences begin. I'm not sure whether the beginnings are different or not.
- I am not sure whether my writing has people talking or not. What is dialogue?
- It is very hard to read aloud. I can't even do it myself.

Recommended Books
for Teaching Sentence Fluency

Remember to ask your students questions like these: *Do you like the sound of this? Why or why not? What would you do to improve the fluency?*

Florian, Douglas. 1997. *In the Swim.* New York: Voyager Books (Harcourt, Inc.). Whimsical, skillfully crafted poems about sea creatures.

Kemper, Dave with Ruth Nathan, Patrick Sebranek, and Carol Elsholz. 2000. *Writers Express: A Handbook for Young Writers, Thinkers, and Learners.* Wilmington, MA: Great Source. Writing process, writers' tips, connections to the six traits, forms of writing, and proofreaders' guides.

MacLachlan, Patricia. 1985. *Sarah, Plain and Tall.* New York: Harper & Row. Wonderful sentence variety. Excellent for dialogue.

Morrison, Toni (with Slade Morrison). 1999. *The Big Box.* New York: Hyperion Books for Children. Excellent for choral reading.

Paulsen, Gary. 1993. *Dogteam.* New York: Delacorte Press. Lyrical, almost poetic prose, ideal for choral reading.

Spandel, Vicki with Ruth Nathan and Laura Robb. 2001. *Daybook of Critical Reading and Writing* (Grade 4). Wilmington, MA: Great Source. A marvelous collage of reading/writing activities.

White, E. B. 1952. *Charlotte's Web.* New York: Harper & Row. Turn to any page for sentence variety. Dialogue? A classic—in a class by itself.

Yolen, Jane. 1981. *Sleeping Ugly.* New York: Coward-McCann, Inc. Snappy, natural, funny dialogue. Excellent variety and flow.

More Ideas

Looking for more ideas on using literature to teach sentence fluency? We recommend *Books, Lessons, Ideas for Teaching the Six Traits: Writing in the Elementary and Middle Grades,* published by Great Source. Compiled and annotated by Vicki Spandel. For information, please phone 800-289-4490.

Spice Up Your Sentences

For use with pages 76–79 in the Student Traitbook

Many beginning writers develop the unfortunate habit of beginning all sentences with the same few words: *My brother is older than I am. My brother's name is Bob. My brother goes to the same school I go to. My brother is really good at baseball. . . .* In this lesson, students are encouraged first to recognize such repetition and then to realize how variety adds spice to writing by making it more interesting and less predictable.

Objectives

Students will recognize repetitive sentence beginnings and revise text to minimize this problem.

Skills Focus

- Listening for varied sentence beginnings
- Discussing how variety affects fluency
- Assessing a piece of text for variety
- Revising a piece of text to increase variety

Time Frame

Allow 30–35 minutes for this lesson.

Setting Up the Lesson

Choose a story students know well—Cinderella, The Three Little Pigs, or Goldilocks and the Three Bears. You can also choose a story that you have read in class or that students have read in class. Ask how the story might sound if every sentence started in the same way. Then, read a "revised" version of the first paragraph or two, making sure you begin every sentence with the same three or four words. Ask students for their reactions. How does it sound? Is it boring? Annoying? Let them know that this lesson is about variety. Varied sentence beginnings add interest. Starting every sentence the same way puts readers to sleep. What response do students want for their writing?

> *Simple, short sentences don't always work. You have to do tricks with pacing, alternate long sentences with short, to keep it vital and alive.*
>
> —Dr. Seuss

Teaching the Lesson

Sharing an Example:
The Cricket in Times Square

Read aloud the excerpt on Student Traitbook page 77, asking students to follow along. It should be clear from the words in color that virtually every sentence begins differently. Ask students to listen and look for the amount of variety and to rate it under "Your Response." Most should see "a lot of variety." If for any reason they do not agree with this assessment, ask them to review the sentence beginnings again to see whether they can find any two alike.

Your Response

After sharing the passage, ask students how they liked it. Was the variety pleasant? How important is it to have sentences begin in different ways?

Revising "Block Party"

Before reading this aloud, remind students that they will be revising for variety, so they must focus on the first few words of each sentence. Read aloud slowly so that they can underline those first words as you go along. If it proves difficult for some students to keep up, read first, and then have students underline. They should notice immediately that there is no real variety here: *We had . . . We called . . . We put up . . . We decided.*

Time to Spice It Up

After students have read their underlined words aloud, discuss the passage as a class. You may wish to rate it in a general way: strong in fluency or weak in fluency. Then let students work together to add variety. Suggest that as a team, they come up with two or more possible beginnings for each new sentence, and then select the one they like best. Also remind them that they can do whatever is necessary to make the revision read smoothly, including combining sentences, adding words, removing words, or changing punctuation. You may wish to list these changes on the overhead so that students can refer to them as they revise: "It is OK to . . ." Beginning revisers are sometimes fearful of "seizing the power," but this is how they become strong revisers.

Share and Compare

Student partners should read their revised sentence beginnings aloud and discuss the impact of the revision. Is it a real improvement? Is it still in need of work? Ask vounteers to share revised paragraphs aloud with the class. Post some of these if you wish.

Extending the Lesson

- Intentionally writing badly is an effective learning strategy. Ask students to select any piece of text from any book they regard as fluent and to "revise" it so that all sentences begin the same way. Ask volunteers to present their "before" and "after" versions to the class and invite comments.

- Ask students to assess a piece of their own writing for variety. Each student should first record the sentence beginnings, listing them on a separate sheet of paper. Then have students rate the variety: low, medium, or high. Next, ask them to do any revision they think is necessary to spice up the writing!

- Ask students to look for especially fluent passages. Have them read these aloud in class, copy and post them to create a collage, or both.

- Post the "Variety is . . ." sayings from "A Writer's Question" in this lesson. It's a great way to help students coach one another.

Just Say No to Run-ons

For use with pages 80–83 in the Student Traitbook

Run-ons are a problem for many readers, who wonder where one sentence ends and the next begins. The run-on problem is *not* a problem of length because a run-on can be short: *I thought it was Don on the phone it was.* Similarly, a sentence can be long yet easy to read, if it is punctuated correctly and written clearly. In this lesson, students will encounter two kinds of run-on problems and practice recognizing and revising each.

Objectives

Students will identify two kinds of run-on problems and use specific strategies for eliminating them.

Skills Focus

- Understanding the concept of "run-on sentence"
- Listening for run-ons in text that is read aloud
- Identifying two types of run-ons
- Revising to eliminate run-on problems in text

Time Frame

Allow 35–40 minutes for this lesson, excluding Extending the Lesson. You can turn this into two lessons by saving the section called "Some Practice" (with Sample 1 and Sample 2) for a second lesson. You will then have two 20-minute lessons, with the actual revision practice in the second lesson.

Setting Up the Lesson

Students are given a good definition of a **run-on sentence** on Student Traitbook page 80. You may wish to take a few minutes to review this definition and the two kinds of run-ons described. If more explanation is needed, model each type of run-on and the way you would revise to eliminate it.

Run-on Problem 1: *The daisies were wilting they needed water.* (Two sentences written as one.)
Revision: *The daisies were wilting. They needed water.* OR *The daisies were wilting because they needed water.* (Add a capital letter and a period, or change the wording.)

Run-on Problem 2: *The daisies were wilting* **and** *so were the roses* **because** *we forgot to water the garden* **and** *so I did not know if the flowers would make it.* (Many connectives hooking little sentences into one BIG sentence.)
Revision: *The daisies were wilting, and so were the roses. Unfortunately, we forgot to water the garden. I did not know if the flowers would make it.* (Dividing the run-on sentence into multiple sentences, and using stronger connecting words—*Unfortunately, we forgot to water the garden*—to link ideas.)

Teaching the Lesson

Sharing an Example: Stone Fox
This fluent example, on Student Traitbook page 81, has been revised to illustrate the two kinds of run-on problems you have just discussed. Students need to hear the samples read aloud as they follow along, but they may need to reread silently to let the text "sink in." Encourage partners to read aloud to each other. Read **Run-on Problem 1** as if it had punctuation. (You will probably need to rehearse ahead of time to do this.) Help students hear, from the way you read, where the periods should go. This makes it easier for them to see and hear that this really is not one long sentence, but multiple sentences.

Read **Run-on Problem 2** slowly and with expression, but do not pause at the **boldfaced** words. Students can pick these out visually and should have an easy time revising this run-on.

Zoom In!
After reading the author's original text, talk about how each kind of run-on affected fluency. Leaving out capitals and periods tends to make text confusing because it is hard to tell where new sentences begin. Putting in many connective words *(but, and, and then, so)* makes the writer sound rushed and breathless.

Some Practice

Sample 1 and **Sample 2** contain no boldfaced hints, so students must determine the type of run-on problem they're facing and how to revise it. As they work with partners, encourage them to read the samples aloud. If you are always the reader, they will not get practice in finding sentence beginnings or adding the right inflection to hear the punctuation. This is not a simple task, but it is an important one. Do not be afraid to let students struggle a bit.

Share and Compare

When the partners have finished their revisions, go over the samples one at a time. Ask what each pair did. Then ask the pairs to read their revisions aloud. Comment on any improvement in fluency.

Extending the Lesson

- Continue the practice with run-on sentences by putting one or two run-ons on the board or overhead each day and asking students to revise them.
- Ask student pairs to create short paragraphs (three to four sentences) with run-on problems and to present them to the class as a lesson. They can read their paragraphs aloud and ask classmates to identify the kind of problem they hear. As an alternative, they can write out the paragraph on an overhead transparency and ask classmates to revise it.
- Create "Wanted" posters for the cagey scalawag "Run-on." The posters should describe "Run-on" as if he or she were a person, using language that defines a run-on. Some students may wish to write in a run-on style to add immediacy and relevance to their posters.

Authentic Conversation

For use with pages 84–87 in the Student Traitbook

Many students enjoy incorporating *dialogue* into their writing, but they sometimes forget that written conversations are effective only when they sound like real people talking. Often, if dialogue does not sound natural, fluency is the problem.

Objectives

Students will use dialogue effectively by making it sound like real conversation.

Skills Focus

- Assessing dialogue for authenticity
- Revising dialogue to make it sound authentic

Time Frame

Allow about 35 minutes for this lesson.

Setting Up the Lesson

Ask your students to define *dialogue*. Many of them will say, "It's two people talking." This definition is not incorrect, but it is incomplete. Dialogue is a record of two people responding to each other and to their situation. Through written dialogue, we learn a lot about the characters in a book or a play.

To introduce this lesson, you may choose to read a strong example of dialogue from a book. (See the list of recommended books on page 78 of this Teacher's Guide.) As you share one or more samples, ask students to let you know whether the characters sound like real people—and also what can be learned about them from the way they speak. Point out that dialogue often reveals a character's mood and also provides clues to the sort of person he or she is. Let students know that dialogue should have a purpose—it should help readers understand something important about the story, the characters, or both.

Teaching the Lesson

Sharing an Example: No Man's Land

Read aloud the dialogue on Student Traitbook page 85. Use plenty of expression so that the conversation sounds as realistic as possible. You may also wish to have two students read the dialogue aloud, each taking a role. This is an excellent warm-up for the second part of the lesson, which calls for revising a section of dialogue with a partner and then reading it aloud.

Your Response

Discuss with students whether the conversation sounds authentic. Is it obvious that one of the characters is an authority figure? Explain.

Authentic Dialogue

This time the example is different. If two characters could sound less authentic than Ian and Detective Schneider, we'd like to meet them. Once again, read the dialogue as dramatically as you can, and ask two students to do a second reading.

Discuss how each character sounds, and what it is about the dialogue that makes him sound this way. Ian is ridiculously formal, while Detective Schneider sounds like a person using his own version of "kidspeak" rather badly. Students should work with partners as they revise. Remind them to read aloud as they go. Suggest that each student take a part, write a line of dialogue, then let the other person respond in character. This approach reinforces the notion of dialogue as a response activity, rather than people talking randomly. Encourage students to think about their characters as they write. What are they thinking or feeling? What kinds of personalities do they have? How can dialogue make these characters come to life?

Share

To judge their own dialogue, students should read it aloud. Encourage them to make changes to make it sound authentic.

Note: This is not a lesson in conventions, so do not put too much emphasis on correct punctuation of dialogue. Let students know you will be doing this as a separate lesson. (We suggest it as an extension.) Punctuation is important, but we do not want students' attention distracted from the primary task of making the dialogue authentic. They may use samples from the text as models.

Extending the Lesson

- Have each student write a dialogue between himself or herself and a character in one of the books being read as a class or a book of the student's choice. The dialogue should have at least ten lines (five lines of speech per character), but it can be longer and can discuss any topic.

- Try a story told completely through dialogue. Ask students to think of a recent situation: deciding what game to play, trouble with a pet, a run-in with a neighbor, a friendly conversation with someone asking for help, a holiday surprise, and so on. Ask them to write the story through dialogue, showing what is happening by what people say.

- Ask students to review any dialogue in their own writing and ask themselves: Does this dialogue sound like real conversation?

- Use a comic strip to show students the importance of dialogue in conveying a message.

- Do a related conventions lesson, showing students how to use paragraphs, quotation marks, periods, commas, semicolons, and so on in dialogue.

Read and Rank

For use with pages 88–91 in the Student Traitbook

A fluent piece of writing is pleasant to the ear and is also easy to read, whether silently or aloud. This lesson focuses on listening skills, encouraging students to read aloud and to listen for fluency. They will be asked to rank writing samples on the basis of fluency, and they will also revise writing to make it more fluent.

Objectives

Students will recognize fluent writing by its sound, and revise a writing sample for fluency.

Skills Focus

- Assessing fluency by hearing a piece read aloud
- Ranking three pieces of text on the basis of fluency
- Revising a writing sample to improve fluency

Time Frame

Allow 35–40 minutes for this lesson, excluding Extending the Lesson. You can divide the lesson into two parts if you wish, ranking samples A, B and C in Lesson 1, and revising "Komodo Dragon" in the second lesson. You will then have two 20-minute lessons.

Setting Up the Lesson

This lesson asks students to do two important things—to read aloud and to listen. The way students read can influence how fluent a piece sounds. You may wish to emphasize this by reading a short passage aloud in two different ways. The first time, read it with little expression. Let it sound flat. Then read it again with expression, bringing out every nuance of meaning. Let students know that when they read aloud with expression, it is easier to evaluate fluency.

Extend the introduction to this lesson by inviting each student to bring into class a favorite book from which to read a brief passage aloud to partners or teammates. Have extra books or passages handy for students who forget. Remind readers to be expressive and to listen for fluency. Listening skills are vital to this lesson.

Teaching the Lesson

Putting Them in Order: Read and Rank

Students will work with partners (or in groups of three) to read Samples A, B, and C on Student Traitbook pages 88–89. Remind them that two readers will read each sample so that the readers will also have a chance to be listeners. Each student will hear each sample twice.

When students have finished reading the three samples aloud, have them rank each piece for fluency. Sample B is the best example of fluency, with lots of variety and closely connected sentences that flow easily from one to the other. It's easy to read aloud. Sample A is so-so. It's a little choppy, but not bad. Sample C, choppy and repetitive, is the least fluent of the three. It is important that each student make his or her own decisions about these samples, sharing and comparing with a partner or partners. Remind partners to read and discuss the samples again if they cannot agree on the rankings.

They should come to agreement within five minutes or so. Open the discussion to the whole class after groups or partners have finished talking, and see how most students ranked the samples.

Sharing an Example: Komodo Dragons

The original of this piece is very fluent, but here it's been revised to eliminate most of the fluency and make it quite choppy. Also notice the repetitive sentence beginnings. Read this revision aloud so that students can both look and listen. It is hard to make this piece sound smooth, isn't it? Remind students to use both their eyes and their ears to decide how fluent this text is.

Zoom In!

When students "Zoom in!" they need to say whether the piece is fluent and to identify any fluency problems they see. The more precisely students can identify problems, the better they will do with revision.

Remind students to read aloud as they work. This will result in a smoother, more fluent final piece. When everyone has finished writing, read aloud the original, and give students time to compare. After they have assessed their final revisions, comparing them to Collard's original, ask volunteers to read their revisions aloud.

Extending the Lesson

- Model your own revision of "Komodo Dragons," and ask students to compare it to Collard's original. Do they think you fixed most of the fluency problems? Make a list of the things Collard did to make his text on the "Komodo Dragon" so fluent. Ask students how many of those writer's tricks they think they could incorporate into their own writing.

- Come at fluency from another angle: poetry. Sneed's paragraph gives us a lot of information about the giant lizards known as Komodo dragons. Ask each student to choose a role and create a poem about the Komodo dragon. Students may choose the point of view of the dragon, of a scientist, or of a person seeing one of these giant lizards for the first time.

- Invite volunteers to read aloud samples of their own writing and to assess them for fluency, saying what is strong and what needs work. See whether the class spots any strengths the writer overlooked.

- Encourage students to read their writing aloud in response groups, listening for fluency. Ask groups to point out strengths, and ask writers to say what could be improved.

Sentence Fluency

Teacher's Guide pages 77, 168–179
Overhead numbers 17–20

Objectives

Students will review and apply what they have learned about the trait of sentence fluency.

Reviewing Sentence Fluency

Review with students what they have learned about the trait of sentence fluency. Ask students to discuss what sentence fluency means and to explain why it is important in a piece of writing. Then ask them to recall the main points about sentence fluency that are discussed in Unit 5. Students' responses should include the following points:

- Vary sentence beginnings.
- Rewrite run-on sentences.
- Make language sound natural.
- Check for smoothness and flow.

Applying Sentence Fluency

To help students apply what they have learned about sentence fluency, distribute copies of the Student Rubric for Sentence Fluency on page 77 of this Teacher's Guide. Students will use these to score one or more sample papers that can be found beginning on page 115. The papers for sentence fluency are also on overhead transparencies 17–20.

Before students score the papers, explain that a rubric is a grading system to determine the score a piece of writing should receive for a particular trait. Preview the Student Rubric for Sentence Fluency, pointing out that a paper that reads very smoothly receives a score of 6, and a paper that does not read at all smoothly receives a score of 1. Tell students to read the rubric and then to read the paper to be scored. Then tell them to look at the paper and the rubric together to determine the score the paper should receive. Encourage students to make notes on each paper to help them score it. For example, they might underline repetitive sentence beginnings or put an X next to run-on sentences.

[Conventions] Unit 6

Overview

In this unit, students learn the difference between revising and editing. They need to understand what each of these important writing process steps requires so that they can tackle both with greater efficiency and purpose.

The focus of the instruction in this unit will be
- emphasizing the difference between revising and editing.
- introducing students to editor's marks.
- allowing students to edit their own work.
- encouraging students to make their own editing checklist.

Conventions: *A Definition*

The trait of conventions includes anything an editor would deal with: spelling, punctuation, usage and grammar, and capitalization. Conventions can also include presentation on the page: general layout; use of white space; formatting, use of fonts for stylistic effect; and the incorporation of charts, graphs, illustrations, although this aspect of conventions is not addressed in this unit.

When students are doing formal publishing (such as creating a book that will be displayed or otherwise shared in a public forum), step in as an editor only after the student has done all the editing that he or she can. Do not step in too soon—let young editors challenge themselves first, even if a few mistakes slip through during practice sessions.

The Unit at a Glance

The following lessons in the Teacher's Guide and practice exercises in the Student Traitbook will help develop understanding of the trait of conventions. The Unit Summary provides an opportunity to practice evaluating papers for conventions.

Unit Introduction: Conventions

Teacher's Guide page 97
Student Traitbook page 92

Students are introduced to the concept of conventions, the last trait.

Lesson 21: What's the Difference?

Teacher's Guide pages 97–99
Student Traitbook pages 93–96

Students explore differences between two vital steps in the writing process: revising and editing.

Lesson 22: Reading the Signs

Teacher's Guide pages 100–103
Student Traitbook pages 97–100

Students are introduced to seven basic editor's marks and begin using them to make corrections.

Lesson 23: The Eye and the Ear of the Editor

Teacher's Guide pages 104–107
Student Traitbook pages 101–103

Students discover that reading aloud and *listening* for mistakes, as well as looking for them, makes an editor more efficient.

Lesson 24: My Very Own Editing Checklist

Teacher's Guide pages 108–110
Student Traitbook pages 104–106

Students begin with personal analyses of their editorial skills, creating checklists to help them remember troublesome conventions. They expand the lesson by creating a poster that specifies editorial skills on which the whole class needs to focus.

Unit Summary: Conventions

Teacher's Guide page 111
Overhead numbers 21–24

Use the rubric on page 95 and the activities in the Summary to practice evaluating writing for clear and correct use of conventions.

Teacher Rubric for Conventions

6
- The paper contains few, if any, errors.
- The writer uses conventions skillfully to help bring out meaning.
- The writer shows control over a wide range of conventions for this grade level.
- The piece is virtually ready to publish.

5
- Only a few errors appear in this paper.
- The writer often uses conventions to bring out or enhance meaning.
- The writer shows control over many conventions appropriate for the grade level.
- The piece is ready to publish with little editing.

4
- Errors are noticeable but minor; they do not impair meaning.
- The writer uses conventions with enough skill to make the text readable.
- The writer shows control over many conventions appropriate for the grade level.
- Editing is needed before publication.

3
- Noticeable, distracting errors *begin* to make the text hard to understand.
- Though much of the writing is correct, errors impair readability in spots.
- The writer knows some conventions but is not yet in control.
- Editing is needed before publication.

2
- Many serious errors make this paper hard to follow.
- Although some of the conventions are correct, serious errors consistently impair readability.
- The writer appears to know a few conventions but is not in control of them.
- Line-by-line editing is required before publication.

1
- Serious, frequent errors make this paper difficult to read or understand.
- The reader must search to find things done correctly.
- The writer does not appear in control of many conventions appropriate for this grade level.
- Careful, word-by-word editing is required for publication.

Student Rubric for Conventions

6
- The reader has to be really picky to find errors in my paper!
- I used conventions to help make my message clear.
- I checked my spelling, punctuation, and grammar. They are super!
- I looked for mistakes, and they are not there. This is ready to publish.

5
- The reader *might* find a few errors, but will not find many.
- I think my conventions help make my message clear.
- I checked my spelling, punctuation, and grammar. They are pretty good.
- I looked for mistakes. I found a couple. It's *almost* ready to publish.

4
- The reader will probably notice some errors. I need to edit more carefully.
- My message is still clear, though.
- My spelling, punctuation, and grammar are *mostly* correct.
- This needs some careful editing before it's ready to publish.

3
- I have too many errors. The reader needs to slow down to read this.
- I did some things correctly. Still, I'm not sure my message is always clear.
- When I read this, I see a lot of errors in my spelling, punctuation, and grammar.
- This could use a lot of editing. It is not ready to publish.

2
- I have a lot of errors. This is very hard to read.
- I did a few things correctly, but mistakes make it hard to understand what I'm saying.
- I made *way* too many errors in my spelling, punctuation, and grammar.
- I need to edit this *line by line* before I publish it.

1
- I made so many mistakes that I can hardly read this myself.
- It is hard to find things done correctly. It is hard to tell what my message is.
- I need to read this aloud, go over it more than once, and get help from a partner.
- I need to edit this *word by word* before I publish it.

Recommended Literature
for Teaching Conventions

No book list is included with this set of lessons because virtually any book can be used to help teach conventions. You may wish to use sections from students' favorite books to talk about writers' skills in using conventions and also to demonstrate how conventions help bring out meaning. An exclamation point shows strong feelings, for instance, and quotation marks indicate speech. Conventions are more than a set of rules to be memorized; it is the meaning behind the convention that counts. As you share published text, be sure to notice

- which conventions authors have used to make meaning clear.
- conventions that may be new to students.
- conventions students would change on the basis of personal style.
- unintentional errors. (There are not many in published books, but they *do* appear—and they are quite common in newspapers, advertisements, mailings, or any publication for which the review/editing process is necessarily very rapid.)

You will also find many lessons, strategies, explanations, and tips to help students work successfully with conventions in the following Great Source handbook:

Kemper, Dave with Ruth Nathan, Patrick Sebranek, Carol Elsholz. 2000. *Writers Express: A Handbook for Young Writers, Thinkers, and Learners.* Wilmington, MA: Great Source. Writing process, editor's symbols, proofreaders' guides, writing samples—everything you need to bring the trait of conventions (along with other traits) to life.

What's the Difference?

For use with pages 93–96 in the Student Traitbook

This lesson is intended to help students understand the difference between *revising* and *editing.* By studying various examples and looking carefully at the kinds of changes editors and revisers make to writing, students come up with their own definitions for these two important parts of the writing process.

Objectives

Students will understand the differences between revising and editing so that they can do each with greater purpose and efficiency.

Skills Focus

- Discussing the steps of revising and editing
- Examining the kinds of changes writers make to writing
- Deciding whether given changes are examples of revising or editing
- Creating personal definitions for revising and editing

Time Frame

Allow about 30 minutes for this lesson.

Setting Up the Lesson

Throughout this lesson, students will work toward personal definitions of *revising* and *editing,* recognizing that these are two separate skills. You might give them an example outside the world of writing, such as building a doghouse. Let's say you finish building the doghouse and say to yourself, "My gosh! It looks like I built this for a Chihuahua, and I have a Doberman. I need to make this MUCH bigger!" Would making the doghouse bigger be more like *revising* it or *editing* it? Now let's suppose you notice that you forgot to paint a tiny spot over the entrance to the doghouse, so you get the paint and fill in that space. Would touching up the painting be more like *revising* or *editing* the doghouse? You do not need to answer these questions for students, and they do not need to answer them yet, but ask them to keep the example in mind as they work through the lesson.

Teaching the Lesson

What's on Your Mind? First Thoughts . . .

Encourage students to write these draft definitions quickly. This is not a test, and they can and probably *should* change their minds as they work through this lesson. Their definitions may change only a little, or they may change drastically. This is a lesson about thinking, so change is good. For now, they should write just what the text calls for: first thoughts. When they have finished writing, students should discuss their definitions with partners and then with the class as a whole. If it seems helpful, record some first thoughts on an overhead transparency, on chart paper, or on the board.

Revising and Editing in Action

The portion of the lesson on Traitbook page 94 works best if students are attentive readers. They must be like detectives, scouting out every change from *Before* to *After.* Then they should record the changes they see and think about what kinds of changes involve revising and what kinds of changes involve editing. Students should notice that in the first example, the detail about parking the car in the driveway was *added,* the order was *changed,* and the part about eating lunch was *taken out.* In the second example, students should note that the missing word *car* was added, the spelling of *first* was corrected, and the *b* in *before* was capitalized.

Revising or Editing: Narrowing It Down

If revising and editing are becoming clear in students' minds, each of the six examples should be easy to define. Here's a tip for students who are having difficulty. They can think Editing = small, Revising = BIG. Editorial changes usually involve such items as putting in a missing word, correcting punctuation, and so on. Revision requires changes such as adding information, deleting information, moving text around, changing the voice of a piece, and so on. Samples of revising on the numbered list include 2, 3, and 6. Each calls for major changes in content or structure. Samples of editing include 1, 4, and 5. These are smaller changes that do not affect the main idea(s) or the way the text is put together. **Tip:** Do not allow students to think that because editorial changes are small, they are unimportant. Emphasize that editing is *critical* to making a text readable.

Share and Compare

Students should compare answers with a partner before you open discussion with the whole class. Find out what students think before giving them the "answers." Ask them to explain their reasons for deciding which items are editing changes and which items are revising changes.

Your Own Definitions

Suggest that students write what they have learned before reviewing their earlier definitions.

Share and Compare

Be sure to share definitions by reading them aloud or posting them. Have student partners compare definitions before sharing them with the class. Have many students changed their minds? What differences do they see now? This is a good time to bring back those brainstormed lists: What do you do when you revise? What do you do when you edit? Would students make any changes now?

Extending the Lesson

- Display a piece of text and make some changes to it. Ask students to tell you whether the kinds of changes you are making are revising or editing.

- Ask each student to review a recent sample of his or her own writing. Then ask them to decide what portion of the changes they need to make will be revising and what portion will be editing. Is it mostly revising? Mostly editing? About the same amount of each?

Reading the Signs

For use with pages 97–100 in the Student Traitbook

In this lesson, students are introduced to seven *editor's marks,* some of which may already be familiar to them; that's OK—this will be a good review! Introduce these marks as an editor's language. Editor's marks are the way editors talk to each other or to writers (or to themselves, if they are making their own corrections) about the mistakes in a piece of writing. Why use editor's marks? Well, think how cumbersome it would be if an editor had to write a little note about each error: "You need an apostrophe here." A caret with an apostrophe tucked inside says the same thing in less space. Editor's marks are a shortcut.

Objectives

Students will learn seven commonly used editor's marks and explain how each one is used in correcting their own or others' writing.

Skills Focus

- "Reading" editor's marks
- Recalling what each mark means
- Using marks to correct text
- Comparing personal text with that of an editing partner

Time Frame

Allow about 30 minutes for this lesson.

Setting Up the Lesson

Because this is a lesson about editor's marks, you may wish to point out that writers use symbols of various kinds all the time. Punctuation, for example, is based on symbols. Ask students what a period means to a reader. Now ask them to think about this situation: If we did not have any punctuation marks, we would have to guess how the writer wanted us to read the text, or the writer would have to insert notes. At the end of a sentence, instead of putting in a period, the writer could say to us, "You need to pause here and take a breath." Instead of a question mark, she could write, "That was a question." It's clear that symbols save time. Of course, this works only when we all agree on what the symbols mean. Think of the chaos at a baseball game if the coach signaled the runner "Steal a base," but the runner thought the coach was signaling "Stay where you are!" The same is true for editing. We all love shortcuts, but editing works only when we all agree on what the marks mean.

Teaching the Lesson

Seven Editor's Marks

Take time to go over each editor's mark in the chart shown on Student Traitbook page 98. The chart shows one example of each mark's use, but you may wish to add others. Use each mark two or three times in various examples on the overhead to explain what each means and describe the correction it is telling the writer to make.

A Little Practice

In the activity on Student Traitbook page 99, students are not asked to correct text; they look at the marks another editor has inserted into faulty text and "read" each mark to interpret the editor's message. What is the editor telling the writer to do? Each student should work independently first and then compare interpretations with those of a partner. Finally, go over the four examples with students. See page 103 in this Teacher's Guide for the answers.

Share and Compare

Be sure that student partners check to see whether they "read" the marks the same way. Ask students for their interpretations before giving them the answers. Make sure that they understand each mark. Model anything that is still bewildering by using it in another sentence.

Put on Your Editor's Hat

Ask students to use editor's marks to edit the copy called "Waking Up." They can refer to the chart if necessary. As editors, their job is to mark all corrections that need to be made.

Remind them that they will not rewrite the paragraph; they are marking the text for someone else to fix. They should read carefully, trying hard to find every error. Suggest that students are on a treasure hunt, but that these "treasures" are not particularly desirable. **Tip:** If students are having trouble, tell them that reading the text aloud to themselves will help.

Check Your Work

Ask each student to work independently first and then to check with a partner. When students have finished, discuss what they have found. Be sure that students tell you which errors they spotted and which marks they used. Then you can put the corrected version on the overhead and go through the errors individually. There are 15 errors in all, and students who find 10 or more are doing an excellent job. It is difficult to spot every error. See Teacher's Guide page 103 for the corrected text.

Nate˅s dog ran out into ^the street.

(The caret with the apostrophe indicates that *Nates* should be a possessive—Nate's. The caret with the word *the* above it shows that a word should be inserted.)

s̲ome of my favorite foods are pizza^green beans^and rice.

(The three lines under the lowercase *s* in *some* show that the first letter of the sentence should be capitalized. The carets with commas tucked inside show that the list of favorite foods should be divided by commas: pizza, green beans, and rice.)

The W̶eather has been a̶n̶d̶ great on our vacation⊙

(The slash through the *W* in *Weather* shows that this should be a lowercase letter. The delete sign through *and* shows that this word should be deleted. The target sign at the end of the sentence shows that a *period* should be inserted there.) **Note:** This sentence could be corrected another way. Instead of deleting *and*, the student could insert an additional word, using a caret symbol: The weather has been *sunny* and great on our vacation.

Don˅t step^in the wet C̶oncrete.

(The caret with the apostrophe shows that *Dont* should be a contraction. The caret with the word *in* above it shows that a word should be inserted between *step* and *the*. The slash through the *C* in *Concrete* shows that this should be a lowercase letter.)

Waking Up

I sometimes have t̶h̶e̶ a hard time W̶aking up. m̲y parents do all kinds of things to get^me out^of bed⊙They open my m̶y̶ curtains gently^call out my name^and my dad will even read to me from a F̶avorite book. They˅re pretty nice about it⊙I guess I˅m just not a morning person. What˅s so bad about i̶n̶ sleeping in?

The Eye and the Ear of the Editor

For use with pages 101–103 in the Student Traitbook

In this lesson, students build on their editing skills by learning to use both their eyes and their ears to spot (or hear) errors.

Objectives

Students will understand that reading aloud helps writers find textual errors.

Skills Focus

- Listening for errors
- Looking for errors
- Marking and correcting errors
- Comparing personal editing with that of a partner

Time Frame

Allow about 35 minutes for this lesson.

Setting Up the Lesson

Remind students that writers and editors work with both their ears and their eyes. Sometimes it is easier to catch all or most of the errors in a piece of writing by reading aloud. You can demonstrate this by reading aloud a short piece or making up a sentence in which you have left out a word or repeated a word. For example, use the sentence *My dog Molly loves chase cars and trucks trucks, too.* See how many students can hear the missing word *to* or the repetition of the word *truck.* Remind them that reading text aloud makes us slow down, so we hear errors that we might not see. **Note:** Students will be using the seven editor's marks from Lesson 22. They can refer to page 98 from the Traitbook.

Teaching the Lesson

Putting on Your Editor's Hat

Here, students put on their editors' hats, which is a way of saying that they "get in the mood for editing." Student writers should feel empowered, not overwhelmed, by the editing process. Empowerment comes from knowing editor's marks, developing expertise in spotting errors, and being in charge of the editing process. The three skills come together as students read the passage "It's that time of year . . ." aloud to themselves. Encourage them to listen and look for errors. They

should use proper editor's marks to note the errors. For misspelled words, they can cross out the word and write the correctly spelled version in the space above. Tell them that you will provide a corrected version for comparison when they have finished.

Check It Out

Students should check their work with that of a partner. Ask them to discuss whether they found the same type and number of errors.

The writing sample on Student Traitbook page 102 contains 11 errors. The corrected version is on Teacher's Guide page 107. Make an overhead of it to share with students as you talk through the errors one by one.

A Bigger Job

This is another practice—one that will provide students with more of a challenge. If students are struggling with conventions, cut this lesson short by asking them to edit only a few lines. Remind students to read aloud and mark any errors they hear or see. Suggest to students that they read the piece twice, and remind them that they will compare work with a partner. This approach is very effective for editing practice. Ask students to use editor's marks. They can refer to the chart on Student Traitbook page 98.

Share and Compare

When student partners have finished marking errors, they should compare their work. Ask students to discuss the number of errors found, whether they found the same errors, and whether they used the same editor's marks. Then discuss the piece as a class.

The piece contains 17 errors. (That is *quite a few*, so cheer for any students who find 12 or more).

Make an overhead of the corrected version on page 107 of this Teacher's Guide and share it with students as you talk through the errors one by one. Point out to students that, as this sample shows, the caret can be used upside down to insert marks such as quotation marks or apostrophes.

Extending the Lesson

- Ask students to use any piece of writing they are currently working on and edit it first by reading aloud, then by inserting editor's marks, and finally by making corrections.

- Ask students to share their work by reading aloud in groups of three. Ask them to listen for repeated words or missing words in one another's text.

Its that Time of year when it seems as though, you can ~~you~~
almost ^hear here the grass grow. we have a day or two of rain,
another day of sun and then it's time to mow. Taking care of
the grass is ^my job. Part of my allowance comes from mowing
the lawn whenever it needs it. At this time of Year, it seems
to need it all the time⊙

The workers across ^the street started early. I think it was 7 A.M.
when the first truck arrived to drop off Lumber. I know that
7 A.M. is not ^super ~~sooper~~ early, but it ^was a day off from school⊙The
noise started with a huge THUD as the lumber slammed
on to the pavement⊙ the neighbors are adding on to ^their ~~there~~
house, so there were big bo^ards,heavy beams, and sheets
of plywood. My other neighbor's dog started barking when
the truck pulled away. ^Because ~~Becase~~ i couldnt sleep anyway, I got
dressed and went outside to ~~and~~ watch.

My Very Own Editing Checklist

For use with pages 104–106 in the Student Traitbook

This lesson encourages students to review their editing skills, honestly assessing their strengths and weaknesses. Every editor is different. One may be strong in spelling but have difficulty with punctuation. Another may be good at everything except spelling. This lesson requires careful analysis of personal writing skills.

Objectives

Students will gain awareness of their editing skills by analyzing their writing and then creating a personal checklist and a class checklist to use as editing references.

Skills Focus

- Reviewing personal editing skills
- Reviewing personal writing to identify strengths and weaknesses
- Listing editing problems
- Transferring what has been learned to a class list or poster

Time Frame

Allow about 40 minutes for this lesson, excluding Extending the Lesson. You can break this into two shorter lessons by doing the personal checklists in Lesson 1 and the class checklist in Lesson 2. You will then have two 20-minute lessons.

Setting Up the Lesson

Point out that all editors—even those who have worked as editors for years—are better at some things than at others. It may be helpful to share some of your own strengths and weaknesses as an editor. For example, perhaps you are an excellent speller, but you use too many exclamation points!!! You might be very good at punctuating, but you confuse *there* with *their.* Explain that the purpose of this lesson is to help students (including yourself as the teacher) identify some editorial "stumbling blocks." Let students know that after each person has identified his or her weaknesses, the class will create an editorial checklist for everyone to use as a reference.

> *The beautiful part of writing is that you don't have to get it right the first time, unlike, say, a brain surgeon.*
>
> —Robert Cormier

Teaching the Lesson

Beginning with You

Students need to look carefully and honestly at their work and identify their editing problems. You might start this process by putting a rough draft of your own on the overhead and inviting students to look for problems—problems you will put on your personal checklist. Encourage students to look through their writing folders and to list up to six editing problems. Point out that it is more helpful to focus on a few specific items than to try to address every problem.

Share and Compare

Use this discussion time to determine whether students can identify the editing problems they have in common. Add your *own* editorial challenges to this list. By doing this, you remind students that even experienced writers have to work at editing.

A Very Classy List

Create a poster-sized checklist that includes from six to eight editing problems that students will work extra hard to resolve for the next month or two. Remember that you can expand or change the list in the future as students overcome present editing difficulties and are ready to address others.

Extending the Lesson

- Update the editing poster regularly as students decide that they have resolved a problem or wish to address a new one.

- Assess materials that you read as a class for conventions. If these items seem to be error-free, remember that assessing for conventions can be an opportunity to note what writers do well. Ask students to identify some of the stengths that their favorite authors demonstrate. They may also point out some areas that could use improvement.

- Find a piece of writing that has a missing word or a double (a word used twice in succession). Read the piece aloud, and discuss with students how much easier it is to hear these errors than it would be to spot them in print.

- Make a bulletin board collage of errors students find in print. How many can they spot? Where do they find them? (If it's something that cannot readily be brought into class, such as a message on a grocery store marquee, students can write the error on paper or print it on the computer.)

ConVentions

Teacher's Guide pages 95, 180–191
Overhead numbers 21–24

Objectives

Students will review and apply what they have learned about the trait of conventions.

Reviewing ConVentions

Review with students what they have learned about the trait of conventions. Ask students to discuss what conventions are and to explain why they are important in a piece of writing. Then ask them to recall the main points about conventions that are discussed in Unit 6. Students' responses should include the following points:

- Understand the difference between revising and editing.
- Use editor's marks correctly to indicate errors.
- Read aloud to hear errors.
- Make your own editing checklist.

Applying ConVentions

To help students apply what they have learned about conventions, distribute copies of the Student Rubric for Conventions on page 95 of this Teacher's Guide. Students will use these to score one or more sample papers that can be found beginning on page 115. The papers for conventions are also on overhead transparencies 21–24.

Before students score the papers, explain that a rubric is a grading system to determine the score a piece of writing should receive for a particular trait. Preview the Student Rubric for Conventions, pointing out that a paper very strong in conventions receives a score of 6, and a paper very weak in conventions receives a score of 1. Tell students to read the rubric and then to read the paper to be scored. Then tell them to look at the paper and the rubric together to determine the score the paper should receive. Encourage students to make notes on each paper to help them score it. For example, they might use editor's marks to note errors in the paper.

The two wrap-up activities in this section are designed for students who have had a chance to work with all six traits of writing. This closure section should not be thought of as a test but rather as a reminder and review and a chance for students to pull all the traits together.

Wrap-up Activity 1 should take about 15 minutes. Activity 2 has four writing samples. All four can be completed as a class activity. Allow about 10 minutes per sample. This will give students time to read the sample, discuss it with a partner, and determine what the *main* problem is. (There may be more than one problem, but one definitely should stand out.) Allow several minutes for a class discussion.

Wrap-up Activity 1

Wanted: Some Traits!

For use with Student Traitbook pages 107–108

In this activity, various traits are represented as characters on wanted posters. Each student's task is to see if he or she can match the name of the trait to the description on the poster. Give students time to read each description, choose a response, and discuss responses with a partner.

Teach this lesson by

- reading each wanted poster description and choosing a response that correctly matches the description.
- checking answers against the Teacher Rubric.
- making any notes about additional issues during class discussions.

After students have completed their work, have them discuss their responses with a partner. Then discuss the wanted poster descriptions with the class. If students do not agree with a response, refer them to specific, relevant lessons or to their Student Rubrics for more detail on a given trait.

Answers: 1. Conventions, 2. Ideas, 3. Organization, 4. Voice, 5. Sentence Fluency, 6. Word Choice.

Making a Diagnosis

For use with Student Traitbook pages 109–112

In order to revise effectively, a writer must be able to read a piece of writing and identify the writing problems. Making such a diagnosis is the first step toward **revision.** That's why this skill is so important.

Teach this lesson by

- reading the samples and answering each multiple-choice question.
- checking answers against the rationales that follow each sample.
- making any notes about additional issues during class discussions.

After students have made their decisions, discuss the samples with the class. If any students disagree with a diagnosis, let them explain why they disagree. Remember, students should be looking for the main problem—but they also may find additional problems. That's fine, as long as each diagnosis can be supported.

Response and Rationale for Sample 1

The main problem with this text is overuse of the words *cool* and *white water rafting;* the answer is therefore **b, Word Choice.** In addition, many sentences begin with *I,* so fluency is also a problem. The message is clear, the organization is fairly strong, and there are no errors in conventions, so the other responses do not apply.

Response and Rationale for Sample 2

The answer should be **c, Fluency.** The dialogue is very stilted. People do not talk this way. It is very easy to see that the characters are discussing softball and they never depart from this topic, so answers **a** and **b** do not apply. The conventions are fine, so answer **d** does not apply.

Response and Rationale for Sample 3

The main problem is **b, Voice.** This writer has lost his dog, but hardly seems at all disturbed. The writer says it was really sad, yet readers cannot feel the sadness. The writer does not tell specifically what he misses about Jake (except that they went on walks), and the overall tone is very matter-of-fact. The conventions are fine, so answer **a** does not work. It is easy to tell what the writer is talking about, so answer **c** does not apply. There are no run-ons in this paragraph, so **d** does not apply.

Response and Rationale for Sample 4

The main problem is with **c, Organization.** The sudden way in which the writer shifts back and forth between the first day of school and the present time is confusing. This is a fairly fluent piece, with highly varied sentence beginnings, so answer **a** does not apply. The phrases *quivering liver* and *rubbery octopus* are just two examples of good word choice, so answer **b** does not apply. The writer definitely does not sound bored; in fact, the paragraph is full of energy, so answer **d** does not work.

Extensions

- Have each student write a letter that tells why it is important that a piece of writing be strong in the six traits. Work with students to make notes about what to say in their letters. Students can then use these notes as they write their letters.

- Invite volunteers to lead a scoring discussion on any Sample Paper for **all traits.** Make sure the volunteers score the paper prior to the class discussion. Suggest that they also make a list of good questions to ask during the discussion.

Sample Papers: Introduction

The purpose of the Sample Papers is to help students view each trait as a whole. By learning to evaluate a piece of writing, students will become better revisers and writers. This Sample Papers section contains copymasters of Sample Papers. There are four Sample Papers for each trait, twenty-four papers in all. Each sample paper is also on an overhead transparency. For each trait, you will find two fairly strong papers and two weaker (in process) papers. The Teacher's Guide will give you suggested scores and a rationale for a particular perspective on every paper.

Using the Sample Papers

You can use each paper alone, for which you need to allow about 20 minutes (the approximate time required to read, score, and discuss one paper). As an alternative, you can use the papers in pairs, in which case you need to allow at least 40 minutes. You must decide whether your students can focus their attention for such an extended discussion. If you decide to use papers in pairs, we strongly recommend that you select one strong paper and one weak paper in order to provide contrast.

It is important to present the traits in the order in which they appear in the Student Traitbook and in the Teacher's Guide. You may, however, present the four papers for an individual trait in any order you wish. Read all four papers for the trait at hand in advance, and decide how you will present them. This will also give you time to know the papers well before discussing them with your class.

In advance

- Read the paper aloud *to yourself* so that you know it well and are prepared to share it with students.
- Make a copy of the appropriate student rubric and the sample paper for each student.

At the time of the lesson

- Remind students about key points they should be looking or listening for in response to a particular paper (trait). Keep this list *short*. (Tips are given in the Teacher's Guide for each paper.)

- Read the paper aloud to your students, using as much inflection as the text allows. Some papers have a lot of voice, and some have very little. Be enthusiastic, but don't try to "invent" voice where it does not exist. (about 1–2 minutes)

- Have students reflect on the relative strengths or weaknesses of a paper. (about 4–5 minutes)

- Ask students to commit *in writing* the score a paper should receive for a given trait before talking to other students. Do *not* share your opinion yet. (1 minute)

- If you use hard copies of the papers, students may be asked to perform simple tasks such as underlining favorite words or circling overused words. Allow time for this before discussing the paper. (1–2 minutes)

- Ask students to compare responses with a partner. Have them answer a question such as, "Why do you think this paper is strong in ideas?" (about 3–4 minutes)

- Lead a full-class discussion. Ask students to justify their decisions: Why did they think the paper was strong or weak? Suggested questions for each paper are provided in your Teacher's Guide. (5 minutes or less)

Sample Papers

IDEAS
Paper 1: The Light Bulb (Score: 3)*
Paper 2: Cookies! (Score: 5)
Paper 3: A Hard Thing to Do (Score: 6)
Paper 4: Something I Am Good At (Score: 2)

ORGANIZATION
Paper 5: Lunchtime (Score: 6)
Paper 6: How to Walk Your Rat (Score: 5)
Paper 7: Not Your Normal Wednesday (Score: 2)
Paper 8: Schools (Score: 1)

VOICE
Paper 9: The Underground City (Score: 2)
Paper 10: Swimming (Score: 4)
Paper 11: Drawing Teddy Roosevelt (Score: 6)
Paper 12: Our New Dog (Score: 1)

WORD CHOICE
Paper 13: Our Field Trip to Wood World (Score: 2)
Paper 14: How a Quarterback Throws a Football (Score: 5)
Paper 15: Why Spiders Have Eight Eyes (Score: 6)
Paper 16: Our Old House (Score: 3)

SENTENCE FLUENCY
Paper 17: A Cool Trip (Score: 2)
Paper 18: Dear Mom (Score: 3)
Paper 19: The Marsh (Score: 6)
Paper 20: Drinking Fountains (Score: 5)

CONVENTIONS
Paper 21: Braids (Score: 2)
Paper 22: How to Make a Skateboard (Score: 1)
Paper 23: Bike Safety (Score: 6)
Paper 24: Night of Terror (Score: 4)

*See the appendix, beginning on page 192, for using a 5-point rubric.

Sample Paper 1: The Light Bulb

Objectives

This paper was selected because it is too general and lacks detail. Use it to show students that writers need a strong main focus and interesting details to support the main idea.

Materials

Student Rubric for Ideas (Teacher's Guide page 5)

Sample Paper 1: The Light Bulb (Teacher's Guide page 120 and/or Transparency 1)

Scoring the Paper

1. Give each student a copy of the sample paper and the Student Rubric for Ideas. Use the rubric to focus students' attention on the key features of the trait of IDEAS—main idea and details. Review that a detail is important or interesting information.

2. Have students think about these questions as they listen to you read the paper: *Does the writer stay focused on the main topic (the light bulb)? Does the writer tell us enough to help us understand how important the light bulb is?*

3. Ask students to score the paper *individually,* using the rubric. They should mark their scores in writing, putting an **X** in the appropriate blank. (If students do not have copies of the sample paper, they can write on separate sheets of paper.)

4. Ask students to compare their responses with those of a partner. They should take a few minutes to talk about the paper and ask each other questions. Expect this process to be slow at first; they will talk more and come to agreement faster as time goes on.

Discussing the Paper

Discuss the paper with the class. Ask students to say what scores they gave the paper and why. The *why* is the most important part in deepening their understanding. Use the following questions to encourage discussion:

• What is the writer's main idea? Is it easy to tell?

• Does everything in the paper relate to the main idea?

• Are the details interesting and helpful in learning about the light bulb?

• Did you learn anything new about the light bulb?

*Rationale for the Score**

Most students should see this paper as somewhat **weak.** It received a score of **3** on the 6-point rubric, though some students may see it as a 2. It has a main idea: *Light bulbs are useful.* However, this is a very general idea and has little support. Many of the things mentioned in the paper—we wouldn't have TVs, computers, or video games—have nothing to do with light bulbs as such. These comments are more related to the issue of electricity (in fact, this is probably the writer's real topic). The writer seems to assume that without light bulbs, we would not have electricity, so we would need candles and torches; this is a big leap. On the positive side, the paper is fairly clear and easy to understand. It is simply too general, and it does not get to the heart of the matter: what makes light bulbs so useful and handy.

Extensions

1. Ask each student to look at a piece of his or her writing. Is the main idea clear? If not, what can be done to make it clear? Are the details interesting? Will additions or changes help?

2. Ask student pairs to revise "The Light Bulb." Encourage them to think through the issue before they write. Ask volunteers to read aloud their "before" and "after" versions.

*See Teacher's Guide page 194 for a 5-point rubric and page 206 for the score.

Sample Paper 1: Ideas

The Light Bulb

The light bulb is a very helpful unit because it gives us light to walk, talk, see, eat, and much more. If we didn't have light bulbs, we would be using candles and torches. We probably would have to carry candles or torches around everywhere.

We would have brick or stone houses with no carpets or wood in the house because torches are dangerous. Candles would be nice. Everyone would buy a dozen candles a month. That would give enough light for the house.

If you think about it, we probably would not have TVs, computers, or video games. That's why I like light bulbs.

Mark the score that this paper should receive in the trait of IDEAS. Read your rubric for Ideas to help you decide.

____ 1 ____ 2 ____ 3 ____ 4 ____ 5 ____ 6

Compare your score with your partner's. How did you do?

____ We matched exactly!

____ We matched within **one point**—pretty good!

____ We were **two points or more** apart. We need to discuss this.

Sample Paper 2: Cookies!

Objectives

This paper was selected because it is full of interesting details that show how well the writer knows the topic. It has a strong main idea and is clear and easy to understand.

Materials

Student Rubric for Ideas (Teacher's Guide page 5)

Sample Paper 2: Cookies! (Teacher's Guide page 123 and/or Transparency 2)

Scoring the Paper

1. Give each student a copy of the sample paper and the Student Rubric for Ideas. Use the rubric to focus students' attention on the key features of the trait of IDEAS—a strong main idea and details. The paper should also be clear and easy to understand.

2. Have students think about these questions as they listen to you read the paper: *Does the writer have a strong main idea (what about the cookies)? Does the writer include enough details to help readers understand the main idea?*

3. Ask students to score the paper *individually,* using the rubric. They should mark their scores in writing, putting an **X** in the appropriate blank. (If students do not have copies of the sample paper, they can write on separate sheets of paper.)

4. Ask students to compare their responses with those of a partner. They should take a few minutes to talk about the paper and ask each other questions. Expect this process to be slow at first; they will talk more and come to agreement faster as time goes on.

Discussing the Paper

Discuss the paper with the class. Ask students to say what scores they gave the paper and why. The *why* is the most important part in deepening their understanding. Use the following questions to encourage discussion:

• Can you learn how to bake cookies from reading this paper?

• What is the writer's main idea? Is it easy to identify?

• Does everything in the paper relate to the main idea?

• Are the details interesting and helpful?

Rationale for the Score*

Most students should see this paper as **strong.** It received a score of **5** on the 6-point rubric, and it misses receiving a 6 only because most of the information shared, though useful and interestingly presented, is known to most readers. Some students may wish to give this paper a 6. This writer is writing from experience and knows the topic very well: buying cookie dough to save time, warming the oven ahead of time, knowing how the dough should feel, using oven mitts to avoid burns, and so on. Of course, if a reader does not wish to read about cookies, the paper may seem less than exciting. But this is not a good reason for lowering the score because the writer presents and explains the topic clearly and thoroughly.

Extensions

1. Ask each student to look at a piece of his or her writing. Is the main idea clear? If not, what can be done to make it clear? Are the details interesting? Will additions or changes help?

2. Score "Cookies!" for the trait of ORGANIZATION—also very strong. Most students should see it as a 5 or 6. (You can hold off on this until teaching this trait specifically.)

3. Ask students to create a how-to paper, based on something they know how to do well. Use "Cookies!" as a model for thoroughness.

*See Teacher's Guide page 194 for a 5-point rubric and page 206 for the score.

Sample Paper 2: Ideas

Cookies!

Baking cookies is SO easy. I can tell you exactly how to do it.

The first thing you do is wash your hands. People don't want dirty hands on their cookies. The next thing you do is put the cookie dough on your working space. Get cookie dough from the store. It saves tons of time.

Set your oven at 350 degrees. If you make it hotter, your cookies will scorch!

After that, open the wrapping on the cookie dough. Now get a spoon and use it to scoop the cookie dough. Take the cookie dough from the spoon, and roll it into a ball between the palms of your hands. It feels smooth, doesn't it? Next, place the dough on your cookie sheet. Do this until there is no more cookie dough.

By now your oven should be ready. Put on two small oven mitts so that you won't burn your fingers when you put your cookies into the oven. Set your oven timer for about ten minutes. Your cookies will be golden brown. Yum!

Mark the score that this paper should receive in the trait of IDEAS.
Read your rubric for Ideas to help you decide.

___ 1 ___ 2 ___ 3 ___ 4 ___ 5 ___ 6

Sample Paper 3: A Hard Thing to Do

This paper was selected because it contains many interesting details that capture the reader's attention. Use it to show that when a writer has a strong main idea and unusual, interesting details, the writing works.

Materials

Student Rubric for Ideas (Teacher's Guide page 5)

Sample Paper 3: A Hard Thing to Do (Teacher's Guide page 126 and/or Transparency 3)

Scoring the Paper

1. Give each student a copy of the sample paper and the Student Rubric for Ideas. Use the rubric to focus students' attention on the key features of the trait of IDEAS—a strong main idea and interesting or unusual details.

2. Have students ask themselves whether details are striking, unusual, or original—or just things everyone knows—as they listen to you read the paper.

3. Ask students to score the paper *individually*, using the rubric. They should mark their scores in writing, putting an **X** in the appropriate blank. (If students do not have copies of the sample paper, they can write on separate sheets of paper.)

4. Ask students to compare their responses with those of a partner. They should take a few minutes to talk about the paper and ask each other questions. Expect this process to be slow at first; they will talk more and come to agreement faster as time goes on.

5. After three or four minutes, ask students to write their reasons for scoring the paper as they did.

Discussing the Paper

Discuss the paper with the class. Ask students to say what scores they gave the paper and why. The *why* is the most important part in deepening their understanding. Use the following questions to encourage discussion:

• Can you tell how this writer feels about making a bed?

• What is the writer's main idea? Is it easy to identify?

• Does everything in the paper relate to the main idea?

• Are the details interesting and unusual—things not *every* writer would think of?

Rationale for the Score*

Most students should see this paper as **strong.** It received a score of **6** on the 6-point rubric because the main idea—making a bed is very hard and frustrating—is exceptionally clear and well supported by unusual details that come from the writer's own experience. This writer shares a clear method for how to make a bed. Anyone who has struggled making a bed shoved against a wall can appreciate this writer's frustration, as well as the writer's innovative solutions to the problem.

Extensions

1. Ask each student to look at a piece of his or her writing. Is the main idea clear? If not, what can be done to make it clear? Are the details interesting? Will additions or changes help?

2. Ask students to write about situations they have found difficult or problems they have solved. Remind them to use this sample paper as a model of how to find a way to solve a problem. Write a "problem" paper yourself, and share it with students when they share theirs.

3. Return to "A Hard Thing to Do" and score it for the trait of VOICE (when you get to this point in your instruction). It should receive a score of 5 or 6; it is very energetic and lively.

*See Teacher's Guide page 194 for a 5-point rubric and page 207 for the score.

Sample Paper 3: Ideas

A Hard Thing to Do

The hardest thing in the whole world for me is making my bed. My mom loves it when I make my bed. I hate it! My bed is kind of big, and it is shoved against the wall where it is very hard for me to go!

For another thing, the bedding does NOT fit! I try to tell my mom this, but she will not listen. "You can do it," she says. I hate it when she says that because the sheets never go on right. They are about one million times too small. I think these sheets were made for some other bed. I can't get them over the corners of my HUGE mattress. Aaaaaaaaah! Sorry—I had to scream there for a second. After about 500 tries, I end up just putting the blanket on top. This covers up the sheet, but the blanket always winds up crooked, no matter how many times I try to make it straight. Then cover up the whole mess with your bedspread. Now for my special finishing touch. Add a whole bunch of stuffed animals. They cover up all the wrinkles! The best thing, though, is to get your mom to make your bed for you. My mom will NOT do it, but maybe your mom will!

Mark the score that this paper should receive in the trait of IDEAS. Read your rubric for Ideas to help you decide. Then write your reasons for the score.

___ 1 ___ 2 ___ 3 ___ 4 ___ 5 ___ 6

_____

_____

Sample Paper 4: Something I Am Good At

Objectives

This paper was selected because it is meandering and sketchy. Use it to show how hard it is to pick out the main idea when the writer addresses many different issues and develops none of them. You can also use it as an example of how "filler" (unnecessary information) weakens writing.

Materials

Student Rubric for Ideas (Teacher's Guide page 5)

Sample Paper 4: Something I Am Good At (Teacher's Guide page 129 and/or Transparency 4)

Scoring the Paper

1. Give each student a copy of the sample paper and the Student Rubric for Ideas. Use the rubric to focus students' attention on the key features of the trait of IDEAS—main idea and details. Students should also check for filler, information that is not needed.

2. Have students think about these questions as they listen to you read the paper: *Does this writer stay focused on the main topic? Does the writer tell us enough to help us understand how important the topic is?*

3. Ask students to score the paper *individually,* using the rubric. They should mark their scores in writing, putting an **X** in the appropriate blank. (If students do not have copies of the sample paper, they can write on separate sheets of paper.)

4. Ask students to compare their responses with those of a partner. They should take a few minutes to talk about the paper and ask each other questions. Expect this process to be slow at first; they will talk more and come to agreement faster as time goes on.

5. After three or four minutes, ask students to write their reasons for scoring the paper as they did.

Discussing the Paper

Discuss the paper with the class. Ask students to say what scores they gave the paper and why. The *why* is the most important part in deepening their understanding. Use the following questions to encourage discussion:

• Does this writer talk about one main thing—or a whole list of things?

• Is there any clear main idea?

• Does the paper contain unnecessary information (filler)? If so, what would you take out if you were revising it?

*Rationale for the Score**

Most students should see this paper as **weak.** It received a score of **2** on the 6-point rubric because it lacks focus and does not develop any one idea. Details are sketchy and limited; the beginning is a list of things the writer does well. The paper also contains filler—especially the references to the sister playing the piano and the writer playing baseball next year. The main idea seems to be "I am good at basketball because I practice," but there is too much unrelated information.

Extensions

1. Ask each student to look at a piece of his or her writing. Is the main idea clear? If not, what could be done to make it clear? Is it focused? Does the paper contain any filler? If so, ask students to revise by deleting the filler.

2. Ask students to give you a topic, and write about it on the overhead. Include some problems as you write—have fun! Ask students to tell you when you wander from the topic (lose focus) or include filler.

*See Teacher's Guide page 194 for a 5-point rubric and page 207 for the score.

name: .... date: ....

Sample Paper 4: Ideas

Something I Am Good At

I am good at a lot of things. I can run a mile. I help my mom cook. I am really good at math and art. My sister plays the piano, but I don't. This year I did a good job in sports. I made about a million points and had some assists. The coach said I did a really good job. I like my coach a lot. My dad came to a bunch of games. In almost every game I made a good shot, and he would really cheer! My basketball has improved because I shoot a lot of hoops after school. I think this has helped me improve. Basketball is my favorite thing to do, next to video games. Next year I am going to play baseball, also.

Mark the score that this paper should receive in the trait of IDEAS. Read your rubric for Ideas to help you decide. Then write the reasons for the score.

____ 1 ____ 2 ____ 3 ____ 4 ____ 5 ____ 6

_____

_____

_____

Compare your score with your partner's. How did you do?

____ We matched exactly!

____ We matched within **one point**—pretty good!

____ We were **two points or more** apart. We need to discuss this.

Organization

Sample Paper 5: Lunchtime

Objectives

This paper was selected because it is well organized and easy to follow. Use it to show that orderly presentation of ideas makes a paper easy to follow; a strong lead and conclusion add interest and complete the paper.

Materials

Student Rubric for Organization (Teacher's Guide page 23)

Sample Paper 5: Lunchtime (Teacher's Guide page 132 and/or Transparency 5)

Scoring the Paper

1. Give each student a copy of the sample paper and the Student Rubric for Organization. Use the rubric to focus students' attention on the key features of the trait of ORGANIZATION. In particular, students should ask themselves whether the paper is easy to follow, and whether it has a strong lead and conclusion (beginning and ending).

2. Have students think about these questions as they listen to you read the paper: *Can you follow what the writer is saying? Do you like the beginning and ending?*

3. Ask students to score the paper *individually,* using the rubric. They should mark their scores in writing, putting an **X** in the appropriate blank. (If students do not have copies of the sample paper, they can write on separate sheets of paper.)

4. Ask students to compare their responses with those of a partner. They should take a few minutes to talk about the paper and ask each other questions. Expect this process to be slow at first; they will talk more and come to agreement faster as time goes on.

5. After three or four minutes, ask students to write their reasons for scoring the paper as they did.

Discussing the Paper

Discuss the paper with the class. Ask students to say what scores they gave the paper and why. The *why* is the most important part in deepening their understanding. Use the following questions to encourage discussion:

- Do you like the way this writer begins the paper (the lead)? Why?
- Do you like the way this writer ends the paper (the conclusion)? Why?
- Is the paper easy to follow?
- Do you think you could use these directions to make a Sophie-style sandwich of your own?

Rationale for the Score*

Most students should see this paper as **strong.** It received a score of **6** on the 6-point rubric because it is easy to follow and includes every necessary step. The beginning is fresh and lively—*I think I'll fix myself a turkey sandwich . . . Sophie style.* The ending works well, too: *Mmmm, it looks tasty!*

Extensions

1. Ask each student to look at a piece of his or her own writing. Are key points and details in order? If not, suggest that students revise by moving things around. Does the piece have a strong lead? If not, the students can write a new one. Does the piece have a strong ending? Again, if the ending isn't working, the students can create a new one.

2. Think of other ways the writer could have started this paper. As a class, write two or three other leads that would work well. Have students suggest ideas for conclusions, too.

3. Create a how-to piece and put it on the overhead, arranging the steps in random order. (Use no more than five or six steps, or this process becomes difficult). Read it with students, and give them time to talk with partners. Then ask them to advise you on changing the order.

*See Teacher's Guide page 195 for a 5-point rubric and page 207 for the score.

Sample Paper 5: Organization
Lunchtime

It's lunchtime and I'm hungry. I think I'll fix myself a turkey sandwich . . . Sophie style.

My brother's baby-sitting me, and he doesn't know how to make a good sandwich. So I guess I'll have to make it myself. I'll need two pieces of bread, a plate, a knife, turkey, mayonnaise, potato chips, and a clean place to work.

First, I have to take the pieces of bread and set them side by side. There. That was easy. Now, I have to take the knife and spread the mayonnaise on both pieces of bread. Good. I didn't have a problem with that. Next, I'm going to take two pieces of turkey and put them on one piece of bread. Now, this is the good part. I'm going to take the potato chips and put them right on top of the turkey. I like to put a lot on. Wow! I can taste it already. Now I just have to put the other piece of bread on top. Mmmm, it looks tasty.

Mark the score that this paper should receive in the trait of ORGANIZATION. Read your rubric for Organization to help you decide. Then write your reasons for the score.

___ 1 ___ 2 ___ 3 ___ 4 ___ 5 ___ 6

_____

_____

_____

Sample Paper 6: How to Walk Your Rat

Objectives

This paper was selected because it is well organized and easy to follow. The lead is strong, and the conclusion works well.

Materials

Student Rubric for Organization (Teacher's Guide page 23)

Sample Paper 6: How to Walk Your Rat (Teacher's Guide page 135 and/or Transparency 6)

Scoring the Paper

1. Give each student a copy of the sample paper and the Student Rubric for Organization. Use the rubric to focus students' attention on the key features of the trait of ORGANIZATION. In particular, students should ask themselves whether the paper is easy to follow and whether it has a strong lead and conclusion (beginning and ending).

2. Have students think about these questions as they listen to you read the paper: *Can you follow what the writer is saying? Does the beginning grab your attention? Does the ending wrap up the writing?*

3. Ask students to score the paper *individually*, using the rubric. They should mark their scores in writing, putting an **X** in the appropriate blank. (If students do not have copies of the sample paper, they can write on separate sheets of paper.)

4. Ask students to compare their responses with those of a partner. They should take a few minutes to talk about the paper and ask each other questions. Expect this process to be slow at first; they will talk more and come to agreement faster as time goes on.

Discussing the Paper

Discuss the paper with the class. Ask students to say what scores they gave the paper and why. The *why* is the most important part in deepening their understanding. Use the following questions to encourage discussion:

• Do you like the way this writer begins the paper (the lead)? Why?

• Do you like the way the paper ends (the conclusion)? Why?

• Is the paper easy to follow? Are any steps left out?

*Rationale for the Score**

Most students should see this paper as **strong.** It received a score of **5** on the 6-point rubric because it is easy to follow and has a strong lead. The conclusion works, but some revision could make it more original. Also, the writer could have put in one or two more details about how to get the harness on the rat. This part starts out well, but the writer has omitted some of the necessary steps. Other details, though, are well organized.

Extensions

1. Ask each student to look at a piece of his or her writing. Are the key points and details in order? If not, suggest that students revise by moving things around. Does the piece have a strong lead? If not, the students can write a new one. Does the piece have a strong ending? Again, if the ending isn't working, the students can create a new one.

2. Try rewriting this paper from the rat's point of view. Does the organization change?

*See Teacher's Guide page 195 for a 5-point rubric and page 208 for the score.

Sample Paper 6: Organization

How to Walk Your Rat

Do you have a rat who hates wheels and doesn't get enough exercise? Well, I have just the thing for you to do: walk your rat. Here's what to do. First, if you don't have a rat or a figure-8 kitten harness with a leash, go to a pet shop and get that stuff. The harness has to be small! Next, gently strap the kitten harness around your rat. To do so, you need the 8 at the top of the rat's back. Hook the leash to your harness and hold it in your hand. Put your rat on the floor—he can't walk if you hold him! Just go around your neighborhood at first. Don't take your rat as far as you would take your dog. Remember, rats have little short legs and can't run for miles. Look at your rat from time to time to make sure he is having fun. When he looks tired, return home, and remember to give your rat some food and water. Enjoy the time walking with your rat!

Mark the score that this paper should receive in the trait of ORGANIZATION. Read your rubric for Organization to help you decide.

____ 1 ____ 2 ____ 3 ____ 4 ____ 5 ____ 6

Compare your score with your partner's. How did you do?

____ We matched exactly!

____ We matched within **one point**—pretty good!

____ We were **two points or more** apart. We need to discuss this.

Sample Paper 7: Not Your Normal Wednesday

© Great Source. Copying is prohibited.

Objectives

This paper was selected because it moves randomly from point to point and the order is not clear. Use it to show that even when the writer tells things as he or she remembers them, the writing seems disorderly if the writer cannot make a connection to a bigger idea.

Materials

Student Rubric for Organization (Teacher's Guide page 23)

Sample Paper 7: Not Your Normal Wednesday (Teacher's Guide page 138 and/or Transparency 7)

Scoring the Paper

1. Give each student a copy of the sample paper and the Student Rubric for Organization. Use the rubric to focus students' attention on the key features of the trait of ORGANIZATION. In particular, students should ask themselves whether the paper is easy to follow, whether it wanders from point to point, and whether it has a strong lead and conclusion (beginning and ending).

2. Have students think about this question as they listen to you read the paper: *Does the writer order the information in a way that makes sense?*

3. Ask students to score the paper *individually,* using the rubric. They should mark their scores in writing, putting an **X** in the appropriate blank. (If students do not have copies of the sample paper, they can write on separate sheets of paper.)

4. Ask students to compare their responses with those of a partner. They should take a few minutes to talk about the paper and ask each other questions.

Discussing the Paper

Discuss the paper with the class. Ask students to say what scores they gave the paper and why. The *why* is the most important part in deepening their understanding. Use the following questions to encourage discussion:

- Do the details seem to be in order?
- Are the actions described in the paper easy to follow, or do you feel lost? When do you first feel lost?
- Do you like the lead (opening)? Why?
- Do you like the conclusion (ending)? Why?
- What would you do differently to give this paper stronger organization?

Rationale for the Score*

Most students will see that this paper is **weak.** It received a score of **2** on the 6-point rubric because the writer meanders from topic to topic with little concern for giving the reader any sense of direction. The lead is very interesting (almost enough to push the paper to a 3), but the reader gets no real explanation of how this Wednesday is unusual. Instead, the writer leapfrogs from bubbles, to a crazy bus ride, to a photo shoot, and then to animal habitats. A strong idea, clearly stated at the beginning, could help keep things more orderly. Right now, it's hard to see how one thing goes with another. The conclusion also needs work.

Extensions

1. Have students work in pairs, to create a revision plan for "Not Your Normal Wednesday." The plan should include at least three tips for making this a stronger paper.

2. Have students work individually or in pairs, and ask them to write brief notes to the writer, commenting (politely) on any problems in organization and suggesting what might be done to fix them.

*See Teacher's Guide page 195 for a 5-point rubric and page 208 for the score.

Sample Paper 7: Organization
Not Your Normal Wednesday

Last Wednesday was not your normal Wednesday. We blew bubbles out of red oak.

Well, it all started on the "crazy" bus ride to the college. When we arrived, we got our picture taken. After the picture we learned about animal habitats and what animals eat. Then came a video about houses and how they're built. There are at least 24 trees in a wooden house!

Then we went outside and watched a sawmill. After that we went to a station about red oak and white oak. Did you know that red oak has holes in it and white oak doesn't? So we got to blow bubbles out of red oak. Then we put rocks into a bucket until a piece of wood broke. I never knew that wood was stronger along the grain.

Then we got lunch! Everyone was hungry. We got two slices of pizza and a soda, free! Then we went to a station where we talked about products from trees, like toothpaste. Then we saw bendable wood—it was cool. Then came the bus ride home.

Mark the score that this paper should receive in the trait of ORGANIZATION. Read your rubric for Organization to help you decide.

—— 1 —— 2 —— 3 —— 4 —— 5 —— 6

Sample Paper 8: Schools

This paper was selected because it moves from point to point without clearly connecting ideas; both the order and the transitions need work. Use it to show how ideas fall apart when the order in a paper is random, and the lead and conclusion are weak or absent.

Materials

Student Rubric for Organization (Teacher's Guide page 23)

Sample Paper 8: Schools (Teacher's Guide page 141 and/or Transparency 8)

Scoring the Paper

1. Give each student a copy of the sample paper and the Student Rubric for Organization. Use the rubric to focus students' attention on the key features of the trait of ORGANIZATION. In particular, students should ask themselves whether the paper is easy to follow, whether it has any identifiable organizational pattern, and whether it has a strong lead and conclusion (beginning and ending).

2. Have students think about this question as they listen to you read the paper. *What pattern does the writer use?*

3. Ask students to score the paper *individually,* using the rubric. They should mark their scores in writing, putting an **X** in the appropriate blank. (If students do not have copies of the sample paper, they can write on separate sheets of paper.)

4. Ask students to compare their responses with those of a partner. They should take a few minutes to talk about the paper and ask each other questions.

5. After three or four minutes, ask students to write the reasons for scoring the paper as they did.

Discussing the Paper

Discuss the paper with the class. Ask students to say what scores they gave it and why. The *why* is the most important part in deepening their understanding. Use the following questions to encourage discussion:

• Do you like the lead? Why?

• Is this paper easy to follow?

• Do you see any pattern in the organizational structure? If so, can you describe it?

• Do you like the conclusion? Why?

• What would you do differently to give this paper stronger organization?

Rationale for the Score*

Most students will see this paper as **weak.** It received a score of **1** on the 6-point rubric because it wanders randomly and does not connect key points to any main idea. The topic wanders from how schools are important to a general discussion of schools. The lead is weak, and the ending isn't there at all; the paper suddenly stops with the comment on how kids get to school. Transitions are missing or weak. There is no identifiable pattern to the organization.

Extensions

1. Ask students, individually or in pairs, to revise "Schools" for the trait of ORGANIZATION. They may add any details or information they wish, as long as each is related to the topic of why schools are important. They may also delete filler.

2. Ask each student to look at any piece of writing on which he or she is currently working and see whether it needs revision for organization. In particular, students should ask themselves these questions: Is the writing easy to follow? Does it have a strong lead? Does it have an effective conclusion? Is there a pattern to the organization?

*See Teacher's Guide page 195 for a 5-point rubric and page 208 for the score.

Sample Paper 8: Organization

Schools

Schools? Why are they important? Schools are important because they are places where kids learn stuff like math, writing, reading, science, social studies, music, art, and P.E. My favorite subjects are art, reading, music, and math. Some schools have everybody sit by themselves, but others have the students sit at circular tables, at tables made from desks, and in rows. You get homework almost every day (not including the weekends). It could be math, writing, or spelling. Most schools have one recess, and some even have two. You get lunch (maybe not on half days). Some kids walk, but others take the bus.

Mark the score that this paper should receive in the trait of ORGANIZATION. Read your rubric for Organization to help you decide. Then write the reasons for your score.

___ 1 ___ 2 ___ 3 ___ 4 ___ 5 ___ 6

_____

_____

_____

Compare your score with your partner's. How did you do?

____ We matched exactly!

____ We matched within **one point**—pretty good!

____ We were **two points or more** apart. We need to discuss this.

Sample Paper 9: The Underground City

Objectives

This paper was selected because it lacks energy. It provides an example for students of how hard it is for readers to remain attentive when a story is presented in a lifeless manner—even if the topic (living in an underground cave) is potentially fascinating.

Materials

Student Rubric for Voice (Teacher's Guide page 41)

Sample Paper 9: The Underground City (Teacher's Guide page 144 and/or Transparency 9)

Scoring the Paper

1. Give each student a copy of the sample paper and the Student Rubric for Voice. Use the rubric to focus students' attention on the key features of the trait of VOICE. In particular, students should look and listen for energy, appeal, some sign of emotion or individuality—a paper that truly stands out from others.

2. Have students think about these questions as they listen to you read the paper: *Does this writer's voice come through? Do you feel as if the writer is talking only to you?*

3. Ask students to score the paper *individually,* using the rubric. They should mark their scores in writing, putting an **X** in the appropriate blank. (If students do not have copies of the sample paper, they can write on separate sheets of paper.)

4. Ask students to compare their responses with those of a partner. They should take a few minutes to talk about the paper and ask each other questions.

5. After three or four minutes, ask students to write the reasons for scoring the paper as they did.

Discussing the Paper

Discuss the paper with the class. Ask students to say what scores they gave the paper and why. The *why* is the most important part in deepening their understanding. Use the following questions to encourage discussion:

- Does the story hold your interest? Did you want to hear more? Why?

- Would you read this aloud to a friend? Why or why not?

- Does this writer seem to enjoy telling this story? What clues do we have about how the writer feels?

- What would make this paper stronger in the trait of VOICE?

Rationale for the Score*

Most students will see this paper as **weak.** It received a score of **2** on the 6-point rubric because it has very little energy. The writer sounds bored and provides only facts. It is hard to tell *how* this writer feels through most of the paper. Also, it's hard to *hear* the voice when the paper is read aloud.

Extensions

1. Have students work in pairs and take turns reading "The Underground City" aloud to each other. Have them decide if it is possible to read the story with much expression. Discuss their responses as a class.

2. Have students list things they could do to make "The Underground City" stronger in voice. Tell them that their lists will become "revision plans" for the paper.

3. Have students gather in groups or in pairs and read their own writing aloud. They should listen for moments of voice in one another's writing, and comment on those parts they think are strongest. (Let writers know they are free to disagree with listeners—but it is helpful to have the response of an audience.)

*See Teacher's Guide page 196 for a 5-point rubric and page 209 for the score.

Sample Paper 9: Voice

The Underground City

Once upon a time there was an underground city. It was very big. There were at least 3,000 families in the city. There were streets and neighborhoods. The biggest part of the city was the downtown section, where the work caves were.

Children started to work after four years of school. Everybody had to work in caves. There was once a cave-in, and 500 people got hurt. I was injured, too. I got rushed to the hospital and was told I had broken my arm. One month later my arm was healed. I was very thankful.

It wasn't fun down there in the caves. People worked hard, but sometimes when the workers were on break they would play catch or kick a soccer ball into a cave.

Worse than the work was the cave itself. It was very dark. There was no electricity. The only light came from the sun through a small hole high above the workers' heads. It was lighter outside, though. That bit of light made us want to find a way to live aboveground some day.

Mark the score that this paper should receive in the trait of VOICE.
Read your rubric for Voice to help you decide.

___ 1 ___ 2 ___ 3 ___ 4 ___ 5 ___ 6

_____

_____

Sample Paper 10: Swimming

Objectives

This paper was selected because it is an excellent example of "in-between" voice. Use it to help students see that a paper can have very strong *moments* (in any trait) even if it is not consistently strong.

Materials

Student Rubric for Voice (Teacher's Guide page 41)

Sample Paper 10: Swimming (Teacher's Guide page 147 and/or Transparency 10)

Scoring the Paper

1. Give each student a copy of the sample paper and the Student Rubric for Voice. Use the rubric to focus students' attention on the key features of the trait of VOICE. In particular, they should look and listen for energy, appeal, some sign of emotion or individuality—a paper that truly stands out from others, or one they might enjoy reading aloud to someone else.

2. Have students think about this question as they listen to you read the paper: *Would you enjoy reading this writing aloud to someone?*

3. Ask students to score the paper *individually,* using the rubric. They should mark their scores in writing, putting an **X** in the appropriate blank. (If students do not have copies of the sample paper, they can write on separate sheets of paper.)

4. Ask students to compare their responses with those of a partner. They should take a few minutes to talk about the paper and ask each other questions.

Discussing the Paper

Discuss the paper with the class. Ask students to say what scores they gave the paper and why. The *why* is the most important part in deepening their understanding. Use the following questions to encourage discussion:

• Can you tell how the writer feels? Where are the clues that show you?

• Are some moments stronger than others? Where are they?

• Would you read this aloud to a friend? Why or why not?

• Does this writer seem to enjoy telling us about her swimming adventures?

*Rationale for the Score**

Most students should see this paper as fairly **strong.** It received a score of **4** on the 6-point rubric because it has strong moments even though it is not consistently strong in voice. It is easy to hear how proud this writer feels after overcoming her fear of water. The sentences "I was doing it. I was swimming!" convey the strongest moment in the paper.

Extensions

1. Have students work in pairs to revise "Swimming" for the trait of VOICE. They may add, delete, or change any details they wish. Ask them first to imagine how it feels to overcome a fear of anything—in this case, a fear of water. Then have them revise the paper so that the strong feelings of the writer come through. Read revisions aloud.

2. Suggest that each student review any piece of writing on which he or she is currently working to identify strong moments of voice. Students should mark these with underlining or with a check. The next step is to see whether the paper can be revised to give it even more strong moments.

*See Teacher's Guide page 196 for a 5-point rubric and page 209 for the score.

name: .... date: ....

Sample Paper 10: Voice

Swimming

One of the times I felt proud was when I got over my fear of water. I lived in an apartment, and I had a pool really close to me. I wanted to swim, but I didn't really know how.

My mom and dad took me in the water with them, and for a while my mom and dad just carried me around. After about 15 minutes of being carried here and there, I said, "I want to try to swim on my own." And my mom said, "Okay, but you can only swim from me to your dad." It wasn't that far, but it sure looked far!

So my mom held me, and I kicked and paddled to my dad and then back to my mom. Then my mom let go! I was doing it. I was swimming! From then on I could swim short and long distances. And so, that is my story on how I learned how to swim.

Mark the score that this paper should receive in the trait of VOICE. Read your rubric for Voice to help you decide.

___ 1 ___ 2 ___ 3 ___ 4 ___ 5 ___ 6

Compare your score with your partner's. How did you do?

___ We matched exactly!

___ We matched within **one point**—pretty good!

___ We were **two points or more** apart. We need to discuss this.

Sample Paper 11: Drawing Teddy Roosevelt

Objectives

This paper was selected because it shows students how even an insignificant topic—drawing a picture—can be lively and entertaining when the voice is strong. Use this paper to show students how much individuality and personal detail contribute to voice.

Materials

Student Rubric for Voice (Teacher's Guide page 41)

Sample Paper 11: Drawing Teddy Roosevelt (Teacher's Guide pages 150–151 and/or Transparencies 11 and 11a)

Scoring the Paper

1. Give each student a copy of the sample paper and the Student Rubric for Voice. Use the rubric to focus students' attention on the key features of the trait of VOICE. In particular, they should look and listen for energy, liveliness, or individuality—a paper that truly stands out from others, or one they might enjoy hearing or reading aloud to someone else.

2. Have students think about these questions as they listen to you read the paper: *Do you enjoy listening to the piece read aloud? How would you describe the voice?*

3. Ask students to score the paper *individually,* using the rubric. They should mark their scores in writing, putting an **X** in the appropriate blank. (If students do not have copies of the sample paper, they can write on separate sheets of paper.)

4. Ask students to compare their responses with those of a partner. They should take a few minutes to talk about the paper and ask each other questions.

5. After three or four minutes, ask students to write the reasons for scoring the paper as they did.

Discussing the Paper

Discuss the paper with the class. Ask students to say what scores they gave the paper and why. The *why* is the most important part in deepening their understanding. Use the following questions to encourage discussion:

- Do you think you might recognize this writer's voice in another piece of writing? Why? How?

- For you as a listener, which were the best examples of strong voice?

- Do you think the writer enjoyed writing this? What makes you think so?

- Do details add to voice in this piece? Where?

- What word(s) would you use to describe this writer's voice?

Rationale for the Score*

Most students should see this paper as very **strong.** This paper received the top rating of **6.** The writer uses a clear, strong voice. The writer also uses detail and humor to put voice into a piece that could have been very matter-of-fact. The writer never sounds bored, though the humor is on the dry side. (Don't be surprised if some scores fall below the 6 level.) Much of the voice comes from the fact that the writer struggles so hard and is unflinchingly honest about the fact that he or she cannot draw well.

Extensions

1. Do a roundtable reading of "Drawing Teddy Roosevelt," in which three or four students have opportunities to read aloud. (This technique works well because this is a longer paper than many.) Tell students to put as much voice and feeling into the reading as they can. Encourage them to make it sound the way they imagine the writer wanted it to sound.

2. Imagine that Teddy Roosevelt were alive and knew how hard this student had worked to get this drawing just right! If he could write a note to the writer, what do you think he would say? Draft a note from President Roosevelt to the writer.

3. Ask students to make a drawing. Then have them write a paragraph describing the experience of drawing as this writer does—one step at a time. Does the detail contribute to the voice?

*See Teacher's Guide page 196 for a 5-point rubric and page 209 for the score.

Sample Paper 11: Voice

Drawing Teddy Roosevelt

"Okay, this is it," I thought, "the worst drawing in all history is going to be right here on my desk." I had to draw a picture of Teddy Roosevelt because I did a report on him and needed a picture to go with it. Unfortunately, he is a hard person to draw, and I'm not very good at drawing.

I started out with the shape of his head. It was pretty good. Then I did his shirt and hair. It wasn't the best hair—it was kind of flat on his head—but it was okay. What next? I thought for a while. I decided to try the eyes. I looked at the picture in the book and saw that Teddy was squinting a little. He also had wrinkles. I made the wrinkles almost exactly how they were supposed to look. I wanted to shout because one thing finally came out right, but I couldn't because I was in class.

I worked on his eyeglasses and nose next. The eyeglasses weren't that bad, but the nose about killed me. Then came one of the hardest parts, his ears. That took me a while because ears are complicated, but I finally got them.

Then came the hardest, scariest, most horrifying part of all. The teeth and mouth! I worked on them forever! It took almost two days. When I got done, Teddy looked as though he needed a major dentist appointment. Before I could get my eraser, my friends saw the teeth and laughed. I just laughed along with them. Then I started all over again.

This time I started with the basic outline of his mouth. I had to make it really big because he had a big mouth and he was smiling. Well, I made it too big. I covered it with my hand so no one would see it and start laughing again. The first chance I got, I erased the mouth. The next time I would do it right, but I had to take a breath.

Finally, I got the top row of teeth done. I worked on the bottom row for about ten minutes. I made the lips and then the mustache. It took a while to get it bushy enough. I was getting the hang of this. I drew a bandanna on Teddy and put polka dots on it. It needed some color, so I took it home to use my mom's colored pencils and give it just the right touch.

It seemed like forever, but at last, I finished it! I was really shouting now! I asked my family how it looked and held my breath. Guess what? They could actually tell who it was! Who knows? Maybe I'll draw some other things right.

Mark the score that this paper should receive in the trait of VOICE. Read your rubric for Voice to help you decide. Then write the reasons for your score.

___ 1 ___ 2 ___ 3 ___ 4 ___ 5 ___ 6

_____

_____

Compare your score with your partner's. How did you do?

_____ We matched exactly!

_____ We matched within **one point**—pretty good!

_____ We were **two points or more** apart. We need to discuss this.

Sample Paper 12: Our New Dog

Objectives

This paper was selected because it shows very little voice or involvement on the part of the writer. This paper helps students see that even a topic with a lot of promise—a paper about a pet—can be lifeless if the writer seems bored or does not put much of himself or herself into the writing.

Materials

Student Rubric for Voice (Teacher's Guide page 41)

Sample Paper 12: Our New Dog (Teacher's Guide page 154 and/or Transparency 12)

Scoring the Paper

1. Give each student a copy of the sample paper and the Student Rubric for Voice. Use the rubric to focus students' attention on the key features of the trait of VOICE. In particular, students should look and listen for energy, liveliness, or individuality—a paper that truly stands out from others, or one they might enjoy hearing or reading aloud to someone else.

2. Have students think about these questions as they listen to you read the paper: *Do you think the writer enjoyed writing about the new dog? How can you tell?*

3. Ask students to score the paper *individually,* using the rubric. They should mark their scores in writing, putting an **X** in the appropriate blank. (If students do not have copies of the sample paper, they can write on separate sheets of paper.)

4. Ask students to compare their responses with those of a partner. They should take a few minutes to talk about the paper and ask each other questions.

5. After three or four minutes, ask students to write the reasons for scoring the paper as they did.

Discussing the Paper

Discuss the paper with the class. Ask students to say what scores they gave the paper and why. The *why* is the most important part in deepening their understanding. Use the following questions to encourage discussion:

• How does the writer feel about the dog? How can you tell?

• Would you want this story to go on for several more pages? Why or why not?

• Do you think the writer enjoyed telling us about the dog? What makes you think so?

• Would you read this paper aloud to a friend? Why or why not?

• What word(s) would you use to describe this writer's voice?

Rationale for the Score*

Most students should see this paper as **weak.** It is tempting to give it a higher score because of the *topic,* but remember: It is not the topic that creates voice, but how the writer *approaches* that topic. The piece lacks energy and detail; that is why it received a score of **1** on this trait. The dog does not even have a name. We know the mom did not want the dog at first, but later she lets it stay. Why? The reader has no idea, nor can the reader hear any of the characters speak. There is no dialogue. The children forget to feed the dog, and this is easy to believe because they do not sound very excited about this new pet.

Extensions

1. Ask students to create a dialogue between the two children or between the mom and one of the children. The issue could be whether to keep the dog, who should take care of the dog, or some other aspect of pet ownership. Students should use dialogue to help bring out each character's personality, remembering to make it sound as real as possible.

2. What if dogs could talk? Perhaps this dog would keep a diary. Ask students to create one, two, or three diary entries from the dog's point of view. Perhaps the first one could be written on the night the dog comes to the house. The next one might be when the mom decides to let the dog stay, and so on.

*See Teacher's Guide page 196 for a 5-point rubric and page 210 for the score.

Sample Paper 12: Voice

Our New Dog

About four years ago my brother was asked to close the garage door, but he forgot. This dog walked up to our garage, and he seemed hungry. We fed him dog food. We still had some left from another dog that ran away from us. Since then the dog has stayed with us. My mom did not want him to at first, but then she let him stay. I am usually the one who feeds him now. My brother is supposed to feed him, too, but he forgets. We both play with him sometimes. He sleeps in the garage, which is where we first found him.

Mark the score that this paper should receive in the trait of VOICE. Read your rubric for Voice to help you decide. Then write the reasons for your score.

_____ 1 _____ 2 _____ 3 _____ 4 _____ 5 _____ 6

_____

_____

_____

Compare your score with your partner's. How did you do?

_____ We matched exactly!

_____ We matched within **one point**—pretty good!

_____ We were **two points or more apart.** We need to discuss this.

Sample Paper 13: Our Field Trip to Wood World

Objectives

This paper was selected because it shows what happens when writers rely on vague words such as *cool, a lot, neat, super,* or *stuff* to get the message across. Use it to show that it is not enough for readers to get the general idea; words must paint a picture in the reader's mind.

Materials

Student Rubric for Word Choice (Teacher's Guide page 59)

Sample Paper 13: Our Field Trip to Wood World (Teacher's Guide page 157 and/or Transparency 13)

Scoring the Paper

1. Give each student a copy of the sample paper and the Student Rubric for Word Choice. Use the rubric to focus students' attention on the key features of the trait of WORD CHOICE. In particular, students should look and listen for strong verbs, sensory words (words that show how things look, sound, smell, taste, and so on), and words that are vague or overused.

2. Have students think about these questions as they listen to you read the paper: *Is it easy to form a picture in your mind? Do you hear any strong verbs?*

3. Ask students to score the paper *individually,* using the rubric. They should mark their scores in writing, putting an **X** in the appropriate blank. (If students do not have copies of the sample paper, they can write on separate sheets of paper.)

4. Ask students to compare their responses with those of a partner. They should take a few minutes to talk about the paper and ask each other questions.

5. After three or four minutes, ask students to write the reasons for scoring the paper as they did.

Discussing the Paper

Discuss the paper with the class. Ask students to say what scores they gave the paper and why. The *why* is the most important part in deepening their understanding. Use the following questions to encourage discussion:

• Are some words used too much in this paper? Which ones?

• How much does a word like *cool* really tell us? What other words could this writer use?

• Do you have a clear picture of these students on their field trip?

• Could you make a movie from the content of this paper? Why or why not?

*Rationale for the Score**

Most students should see this paper as **weak.** The words *cool, a lot,* and *super* are used far too much; and because they are imprecise, readers do not get a very clear picture of events. There are no strong verbs, and no sensory language to paint a picture in the reader's mind. Consequently, the score in the trait of WORD CHOICE is **2.** Some students may see the paper as a 1, though we think it's somewhat stronger than that because the general message comes through.

Extensions

1. Ask students to revise "Our Field Trip to Wood World" for word choice, eliminating every instance of *cool, a lot,* and *super*. They can work with partners and brainstorm alternatives. Read the results aloud and compare them to the original.

2. Have each student look at a piece of his or her own writing and underline any words that are weak or overused. Ask students to brainstorm, on their own or with a partner, words more descriptive and precise. See what this revision does for the overall sound of the paper.

*See Teacher's Guide page 197 for a 5-point rubric and page 210 for the score.

Sample Paper 13: Word Choice

Our Field Trip to Wood World

Last Wednesday my class and I went to Wood World, and it was cool. Then we saw a piece of wood with no bark because a beaver had eaten it. It was cool. I was happy. Then we saw a movie. I liked it a lot. I liked the sawmill a lot, too. Then we saw some super-strong wood. I liked it a lot. It took 60 pounds to break the wood. It was cool. Lunch was my favorite part. We had pizza. The bendable wood was super cool. Then we went back home.

Mark the score that this paper should receive in the trait of WORD CHOICE. Read your rubric for Word Choice to help you decide. Then write the reasons for your score.

___ 1 ___ 2 ___ 3 ___ 4 ___ 5 ___ 6

_____

_____

_____

Compare your score with your partner's. How did you do?

___ We matched exactly!

___ We matched within **one point**—pretty good!

___ We were **two points or more** apart. We need to discuss this.

Sample Paper 14: How a Quarterback Throws a Football

Objectives

This paper was selected because the writer makes good use of verbs. Strong verbs make the writing precise, lively, and interesting. This is a good model for students.

Materials

Student Rubric for Word Choice (Teacher's Guide page 59)

Sample Paper 14: How a Quarterback Throws a Football (Teacher's Guide page 160 and/or Transparency 14)

Scoring the Paper

1. Give each student a copy of the sample paper and the Student Rubric for Word Choice. Use the rubric to focus students' attention on the key features of the trait of WORD CHOICE. In particular, students should look and listen for strong verbs, sensory words (words that show how things look, sound, smell, taste, and feel), and words that are vague or overused.

2. Have students think about these questions as they listen to you read the paper: *What words help you see a picture in your mind? Are any words overused?*

3. Ask students to score the paper *individually,* using the rubric. They should mark their scores in writing, putting an **X** in the appropriate blank. (If students do not have copies of the sample paper, they can write on separate sheets of paper.)

4. Ask students to compare their responses with those of a partner. They should take a few minutes to talk about the paper and ask each other questions.

Discussing the Paper

Discuss the paper with the class. Ask students to say what scores they gave the paper and why. The *why* is the most important part in deepening their understanding. Use the following questions to encourage discussion:

• Which words in this paper did you find most lively and interesting?

• Did you notice any strong verbs? Name them.

• Are any words overused? If so, which ones?

• Which words help you picture what is happening on the football field?

*Rationale for the Score**

Most students should see this paper as **strong.** It received a **5** on the 6-point rubric. Some students may vote to give the paper a 6. We would have given it a 6 if the first few sentences were as strong as the rest; there was a lot of "lining up on the line!" Still, the first few sentences are clear, and precise words are used. The writer makes extensive use of verbs, especially in the second part of the paper: *drops back, seeks, rotates, gets sacked, steps forward, follows through, score, scream, celebrate.* The writing is clean and concise, free of extraneous words. It is easy to picture what is happening, even if you do not know much about football.

Extensions

1. Start with any piece of writing in which the verbs are strong. You may wish to write a sample yourself or borrow from a favorite piece of literature. Remove each strong verb, and replace it with a tired, less exciting verb. Then, put the result on the overhead. See whether students can replace each of the weak verbs. Compare the finished piece to the original.

2. Have each student look at a piece of his or her writing and underline any weak verbs. Ask students to underline passages where strong verbs would add some energy, and have them do some revising. Each writer should try to make at least four changes.

3. Make a poster listing favorite verbs, nouns, and modifiers. You can begin by scanning "How a Quarterback Throws a Football"—but keep adding to the lists as you read new pieces.

*See Teacher's Guide page 197 for a 5-point rubric and page 210 for the score.

name: .... date: ....

How a Quarterback Throws a Football

You all probably know what football is. But did you ever wonder how a quarterback throws a football? Well, it goes like this.

First, the coach tells the play to the quarterback, and the quarterback tells the team. Then the team lines up on the line of scrimmage. The quarterback lines up behind the center, who lines up in the middle of the line of scrimmage.

The quarterback then calls out, "Down set hut hut!" And the center hikes the ball (gives the ball) to the quarterback. Then the quarterback drops back and rotates his hand on the ball to get his position on the laces (but he has to be careful of the defense because he might get sacked). Then, while he is rotating his hand on the ball, he seeks an open receiver (a person who catches the ball). When he finds an open receiver, he pulls his arm back, steps forward with his opposite foot, and follows through on his throw in the direction of the receiver. If the pass is good, the receiver will catch the ball and run for a touchdown. If he scores, the team and the crowd scream and celebrate.

Mark the score that this paper should receive in the trait of WORD CHOICE. Read your rubric for Word Choice to help you decide.

___ 1 ___ 2 ___ 3 ___ 4 ___ 5 ___ 6

Sample Paper 15: Why Spiders Have Eight Eyes

Objectives

This paper was selected because it reflects the power of strong verbs, sensory words, and precise language in general. Use this paper to show the power of carefully chosen words.

Materials

Student Rubric for Word Choice (Teacher's Guide page 59)

Sample Paper 15: Why Spiders Have Eight Eyes (Teacher's Guide pages 163–164 and/or Transparencies 15 and 15a)

Scoring the Paper

1. Give each student a copy of the sample paper and the Student Rubric for Word Choice. Use the rubric to focus students' attention on the key features of the trait of WORD CHOICE. In particular, students should look and listen for favorite words, strong verbs, sensory words (words that show how things look, sound, smell, taste, or feel), or any words that are vague or overused.

2. Have students think about these questions as they listen to you read the paper: *What words do you like in this piece? What strong verbs do you hear?*

3. Ask students to score the paper *individually,* using the rubric. They should mark their scores in writing, putting an **X** in the appropriate blank. (If students do not have copies of the sample paper, they can write on separate sheets of paper.)

4. Ask students to compare their responses with those of a partner. They should take a few minutes to talk about the paper and ask each other questions.

Discussing the Paper

Discuss the paper with the class. Ask students to say what scores they gave the paper and why. The *why* is the most important part in deepening their understanding. Use the following questions to encourage discussion:

• Which words are your favorites in this paper?

• Do you notice any strong verbs? Name them.

• Can you picture Spider after he took all the eyes from other creatures?

• Could you make a film of this fable? Who would do the voice of Spider?

*Rationale for the Score**

Most students should see this paper as **strong.** It received a **6** on the 6-point rubric. It has strong verbs, precise language, and many good sensory details: the animals feel *exhausted,* Spider feels *selfish,* Spider *crunches* as he devours Mouse. The phrasing is explicit: *flew into a rage,* for example. Modifiers are used well, too: *gruesome, exhausted,* and *selfish* are clear and exact. Students should have little trouble finding favorite words and phrases.

Extensions

1. Ask students to create a dialogue between Spider and one of the other animals. Tell them to be sure that the dialogue sounds like real speech.

2. Have each student draw a picture of Spider covered with his stolen eyes. Encourage students to imagine their pictures being used in a book about Spider.

3. Spider probably isn't very happy with the outcome of this story. At the end, he is tiny, with most animals, except insects, too large to feed upon. How does he feel about that? Ask students to create a journal entry as Spider might write it, expressing his feelings. They should focus on good sensory details and strong verbs. Read the results aloud.

*See Teacher's Guide page 197 for a 5-point rubric and page 211 for the score.

name: .... date: ....

Sample Paper 15: Word Choice

Why Spiders Have Eight Eyes

Long ago, long before even dinosaurs were alive, there was Spider and all the other creatures we have today. Spider was the biggest creature of all, and he could do anything to the other creatures whenever he wanted. One day, Spider woke up from a deep sleep, and he was feeling very selfish. He thought about the dream he had just had. He dreamed that he could see only ahead of himself, and when he wanted to see something on the side, he had to turn around! He thought, "Since I am so mighty, I shouldn't have to do all the work!" So he made all the other creatures carry him wherever he wanted to go and turn him around whenever he wanted to look at something. He liked this so much that he made the animals gather his food, too! After a year or so, all the animals were exhausted and wouldn't work for Spider anymore.

Spider flew into a rage. "Unless you work for me right now, I'll eat you all up!" he said. Nobody answered him. "Fine! Be that way!" yelled Spider. "I'm hungry anyway!" And with that, Spider picked up Mouse by the tail. He was about to eat him when BOOM! An idea hit him in the head. He would save Mouse's eyes and put them on his own body so that he wouldn't have to turn around anymore! So Spider plopped Mouse in his mouth, "Crunch, crunch!" and carefully picked out the eyes. He stuck them on his body and repeated the same steps until all the animals were gone. He was satisfied only when his whole body was covered with eyes. What a gruesome sight Spider was! Spider didn't care that all the animals were gone because now he could see! He could see the blue sky, green trees, golden sun, white clouds, gray stones, and all these wonderful things at once!

The next day Spider went out to look for some food, but he soon realized that he didn't know which plants were good and which plants were bad. So he called to the Leader of All Animals, "The food has run low! Please send me some more!"

The Leader replied, "No, first give back the animals' eyes!"

"How?" asked Spider.

"Put them on this rock!" said the Leader.

"Fine!" said Spider.

So Spider went to the nearest rock and put down the eyes, although very reluctantly. But because Spider was so greedy, he kept eight eyes to himself. Because Spider gave some of the eyes back, the Leader of All Animals kept his promise and gave Spider some food. The Leader made sure that everything was bigger than Spider except the insects. That's why Spider's prey are all insects, and that's why Spider has eight eyes.

Mark the score that this paper should receive in the trait of WORD CHOICE. Read your rubric for Word Choice to help you decide.

___ 1 ___ 2 ___ 3 ___ 4 ___ 5 ___ 6

Sample Paper 16: Our Old House

Objectives

This paper was selected because the piece lacks energy and liveliness. Use it to show students that overuse of words like *cool, stuff, really, super, neat,* and so on makes writing inexact and boring.

Materials

Student Rubric for Word Choice (Teacher's Guide page 59)

Sample Paper 16: Our Old House (Teacher's Guide page 167 and/or Transparency 16)

Scoring the Paper

1. Give each student a copy of the sample paper and the Student Rubric for Word Choice. Use the rubric to focus students' attention on the key features of the trait of WORD CHOICE. In particular, they should look and listen for strong verbs, sensory words (words that show how things look, sound, smell, taste, and feel), and words that are vague or overused.

2. Have students think about this question as they listen to you read the paper: *What would you say about this writer's choice of words?*

3. Ask students to score the paper *individually,* using the rubric. They should mark their scores in writing, putting an **X** in the appropriate blank. (If students do not have copies of the sample paper, they can write on separate sheets of paper.)

4. Ask students to compare their responses with those of a partner. They should take a few minutes to talk about the paper and ask each other questions.

5. After three or four minutes, ask students to write the reasons for scoring the paper as they did.

Discussing the Paper

Discuss the paper with the class. Ask students to say what scores they gave the paper and why. The *why* is the most important part in deepening their understanding. Use the following questions to encourage discussion:

- Can you picture the house and yard? What words help you do that?
- Are any words used too much? Which ones? What other words could we substitute?
- Do some words sound tired? Which ones are tired words?
- Could you make a picture of the writer's room just from the description? Why or why not?

Rationale for the Score*

Most students will decide that this paper is **weak.** It received a **3** on the 6-point rubric. It is clear in a general sense but lacks flair. The verbs are weak, and many words are vague or overused: *neat, cool, really,* and so on. The language needs an energy boost!

Extensions

1. Ask students to imagine that the author of "Why Spiders Have Eight Eyes" is going to rewrite "Our Old House." What might it sound like? Have students work in pairs to rewrite "Our Old House." Encourage them to let wonderful words fly!

2. Have students create a dialogue between the writer of "Why Spiders Have Eight Eyes" and the writer of "Our Old House." Suggest that the writers meet at lunch or after school. Perhaps one wants advice on a new book to read, perhaps they cook up a delicious, interesting dinner together, or discuss what to do for fun. Ask students to give the two writers names. Then, in the dialogue, have them speak using the same kinds of language they used in their writing. They should sound very different! Read results aloud.

3. Make a class poster of "Tired Words." Start the collection with a few worn phrases from "Our Old House," but keep adding to it as students make suggestions or trite words and phrases occur in your reading.

*See Teacher's Guide page 197 for a 5-point rubric and page 211 for the score.

Sample Paper 16: Word Choice

Our Old House

I miss our old house a lot. It was so neat. It had a red front door that was very pretty. We had a lot of trees and things in our yard, so it was really shady a lot of the time. We could play outside and stuff and not get too hot. I liked my room. It was a very nice room that was just the right size with bunk beds in one corner. It had this super neat carpet and space to keep tons of stuff. My dog usually slept in my room, but a lot of times he slept on the front porch. In our backyard we had this one really big tree I liked to climb. It had branches strong enough to hold you up so you would not fall.

Mark the score that this paper should receive in the trait of WORD CHOICE. Read your rubric for Word Choice to help you decide. Then write the reasons for your score.

_____ 1 _____ 2 _____ 3 _____ 4 _____ 5 _____ 6

_____

_____

_____

Compare your score with your partner's. How did you do?

_____ We matched exactly!

_____ We matched within **one point**—pretty good!

_____ We were **two points or more** apart. We need to discuss this.

Sentence Fluency

Sample Paper 17: A Cool Trip

Objectives

This paper was selected because it illustrates two common Sentence Fluency problems: run-ons and repetitive sentence beginnings. Use the paper to help students see the impact of these problems on the overall rhythm and flow of the language.

Materials

Student Rubric for Sentence Fluency (Teacher's Guide page 77)

Sample Paper 17: A Cool Trip (Teacher's Guide page 170 and/or Transparency 17)

Scoring the Paper

1. Give each student a copy of the sample paper and the Student Rubric for Sentence Fluency. Use the rubric to focus students' attention on the key features of the trait of sentence fluency. In particular, students should look and listen for sentence beginnings, run-ons, and a general, smooth flow that's easy on the ear.

2. Have students think about this question as they listen to you read the paper: *Does the writing sound smooth when read aloud?*

3. Ask students to score the paper *individually,* using the rubric. They should mark their scores in writing, putting an **X** in the appropriate blank. (If students do not have copies of the sample paper, they can write on separate sheets of paper.)

4. Ask students to compare their responses with those of a partner. They should take a few minutes to talk about the paper and ask each other questions.

5. After three or four minutes, ask students to write the reasons for scoring the paper as they did.

Discussing the Paper

Discuss the paper with the class. Ask students to say what scores they gave the paper and why. The *why* is the most important part in deepening their understanding. Use the following questions to encourage discussion:

- As you looked at and listened to this paper, what did you notice about the sentence beginnings? Did this help or hurt the fluency?

- Did you notice any run-on sentences? Did they help or hurt the fluency?

- If you read this paper aloud, did you find it hard to read? Why?

Rationale for the Score

Most students should see this paper as **weak.** It received a **2** on the 6 point rubric because it has repetitive sentence beginnings and several run-on sentences. It is awkward to read aloud. Eliminating the run-ons and varying the sentence beginnings would make the writing smoother and easier to read.

Extensions

1. This is a good paper to revise as a class. Work on one problem at a time. First, ask students to tell you which sentences are run-ons, and have them suggest ways to revise them. Then, work on sentence beginnings. You can brainstorm two or three possibilities, and then settle on the one the class likes best. Finally, read the revised piece aloud. You should hear a great improvement.

2. Ask students to choose a simple topic a day with a pet, a shopping adventure, a problem solved, a favorite (or least favorite) meal—and to write a short paragraph (4–6 sentences). Tell students to begin each sentence in a different way. Read the results aloud. Write a paragraph yourself making sure that two sentence beginnings are identical. See whether your student critics can hear the duplication when you read your work aloud.

*See Teacher's Guide page 198 for a 5-point rubric and page 211 for the score.

Sample Paper 17: Sentence Fluency

A Cool Trip

Last fall we went on a trip. We got our picture taken just before we left our driveway it was right by our car. We drove in our car from California to about Iowa. We saw some mountains they were pretty big. We saw three movies and we ate in a ton of restaurants and some of the food was pretty good but not all of it was that good. We got to see a waterfall and a herd of buffalo. This one time we got to stay in this motel it had a swimming pool with its own waterfall at one end. We got hundreds of mosquito bites. Then we went back to school. Then we wished we were still on vacation!

Mark the score that this paper should receive in the trait of SENTENCE FLUENCY. Read your rubric for Sentence Fluency to help you decide. Then write the reasons for your score.

____ 1 ____ 2 ____ 3 ____ 4 ____ 5 ____ 6

_____

_____

_____

Compare your score with your partner's. How did you do?

____ We matched exactly!

____ We matched within **one point**—pretty good!

____ We were **two points or more** apart. We need to discuss this.

Sample Paper 18: Dear Mom

Objectives

This paper was selected because it illustrates some Sentence Fluency problems. It is quite choppy, all sentences are about the same length, and it has repetitive sentence beginnings. Use the paper to help students see the impact of these problems on the overall rhythm and flow of the language.

Materials

Student Rubric for Sentence Fluency (Teacher's Guide page 77)

Sample Paper 18: Dear Mom (Teacher's Guide page 173 and/or Transparency 18)

Scoring the Paper

1. Give each student a copy of the sample paper and the Student Rubric for Sentence Fluency. Use the rubric to focus students' attention on the key features of the trait of SENTENCE FLUENCY. In particular, students should look and listen for differences in sentence beginnings and sentence lengths, run-ons, and a general smooth flow that's easy on the ear.

2. Have students think about these questions as they listen to you read the paper: *Do the sentence lengths vary? How would you describe the overall flow?*

3. Ask students to score the paper *individually,* using the rubric. They should mark their scores in writing, putting an **X** in the appropriate blank. (If students do not have copies of the sample paper, they can write on separate sheets of paper.)

4. Ask students to compare their responses with those of a partner. They should take a few minutes to talk about the paper and ask each other questions.

5. After three or four minutes, ask students to write the reasons for scoring the paper as they did.

Discussing the Paper

Discuss the paper with the class. Ask students to say what scores they gave the paper and why. The *why* is the most important part in deepening their understanding. Use the following questions to encourage discussion:

- As you looked at and listened to this paper, what did you notice about the sentence beginnings? Did this help or hurt the fluency?

- Did you think the paper sounded smooth when you heard it read aloud? Was it a little choppy? What's the cure for choppy sentences?

- If you have read the paper called "A Cool Trip," compare it to "Dear Mom" for fluency. Which one is more fluent? Why?

Rationale for the Score*

Students should see this paper as somewhat **weak.** It recieved a **3** on the 6-point rubric because the writer repeatedly uses *It, I* or *You* as a sentence opener. In addition, the overall piece is choppy because sentences tend to be short and about the same length. Some sentence combining would help.

Extensions

1. Have students work in pairs to revise this piece to achieve a smoother flow. Then have them revise by combining choppy sentences to make longer, flowing sentences. Have students read the results aloud.

2. You can also ask students to revise sentence beginnings. Though this piece is not as repetitive as "A Cool Trip," it could use some variety. Ask students to make the beginnings more interesting.

3. Suppose Mom responded to this letter. What might she say? Ask students to compose a letter from Mom to the writer, making sure to vary sentence beginnings and lengths. Read some papers aloud to hear the fluency.

4. Imagine a discussion between Mom and the writer once Mom has received this letter. What might they say to each other? Ask students to write a dialogue, with each character having *at least four lines* (partners can work together to complete this activity). Remind students to make the dialogue as natural as possible. It helps to think about what each character is like and what each one wants.

*See Teacher's Guide page 198 for a 5-point rubric and page 212 for the score.

Sample Paper 18: Sentence Fluency

Dear Mom

Dear Mom,

You know it would be nice to have a laptop. If you got me a laptop for my birthday, it would help with school and writing. I could practice writing stories, and I could use it when doing my homework. It would be fun to put it in my room. You could borrow it when you need it. It would help you with your work. You would not have to go to Dad's office to send an e-mail! You could send it from home. I would not be on it all day. And I would share it with Billy, too! I can see that smile on your face. I can tell you are thinking about getting me a laptop. I hope to get a laptop for my birthday!

Mark the score that this paper should receive in the trait of SENTENCE FLUENCY. Read your rubric for Sentence Fluency to help you decide. Then write the reasons for your score.

____ 1 ____ 2 ____ 3 ____ 4 ____ 5 ____ 6

_____

_____

_____

Compare your score with your partner's. How did you do?

____ We matched exactly!

____ We matched within **one point**—pretty good!

____ We were **two points or more** apart. We need to discuss this.

Sample Paper 19: The Marsh

Objectives

This paper was selected because its smooth, natural sound models fluency well. Use it to show students how well-crafted, varied sentences can create a smooth sound that is pleasing to the ear.

Materials

Student Rubric for Sentence Fluency (Teacher's Guide page 77)

Sample Paper 19: The Marsh (Teacher's Guide page 176 and/or Transparency 19)

Scoring the Paper

1. Give each student a copy of the sample paper and the Student Rubric for Sentence Fluency. Use the rubric to focus students' attention on the key features of the trait of SENTENCE FLUENCY. In particular, students should look and listen for differences in sentence beginnings and sentence lengths, run-ons, and a smooth flow of words.

2. Have students think about these questions as they listen to you read the paper: *Does the writer vary the sentences? Does the piece sound smooth when you hear it read aloud?*

3. Ask students to score the paper *individually,* using the rubric. They should mark their scores in writing, putting an **X** in the appropriate blank. (If students do not have copies of the sample paper, they can write on separate sheets of paper.)

4. Ask students to compare their responses with those of a partner. They should take a few minutes to talk about the paper and ask each other questions.

Discussing the Paper

Discuss the paper with the class. Ask students to say what scores they gave the paper and why. The *why* is the most important part in deepening their understanding. Use the following questions to encourage discussion:

- As you looked and listened to this paper, what did you notice about the sentence beginnings? Did this help or hurt the fluency?

- Did you think the paper sounded smooth when you heard it read aloud?

- Do you think reading this paper aloud would be easy or hard? Why do you think so?

- Does the dialogue in this piece sound natural? Why or why not?

*Rationale for the Score**

Most students should see this paper as very **strong.** It received a **6** on the 6-point rubric because virtually all sentences begin differently, it has no fluency problems, and the sound is smooth. It's a pleasure to read aloud. In addition, the dialogue sounds authentic. This piece has a natural sound that makes it a good model for fluency.

Extensions

1. Ask two or three volunteers to read "The Marsh" aloud. Have the rest of the class close their eyes and listen. What do they hear? Is it fluent?

2. Have students read pieces of their own writing to one another in response groups. They should listen *only for the fluency*. Remind them to pay attention to sentence beginnings and lengths. They should NOT hear any run-ons.

3. What if the dialogue between the writer and the dad were extended? Ask students to create a longer conversation that occurs just following a visit to the marsh. Perhaps the characters see something they both like—or something they have not seen before. Each character should have *at least four lines*. Students can work on this in pairs, with each student creating the lines for one character. Ask volunteers to read their dialogue aloud and listen for authenticity.

*See Teacher's Guide page 198 for a 5-point rubric and page 212 for the score.

Sample Paper 19: Sentence Fluency

The Marsh

Near our house is a marsh where a lot of wild animals live. If you walk past quietly, you will see geese nesting. Or, if you're very lucky, you might see an otter just poking his nose out of the water. He might be looking for his evening meal of fish. My favorite things to see at the marsh are the blackbirds. They sing in a way that is different from any other bird. It sounds a little like singing, but a little like a whistle, too. Once my dad found a huge brown toad just hopping his way home across the path. A lot of people pick up toads or other small creatures when they find them, but Dad said that was not a good idea. "Wild creatures should go free," he told me. "You're right," I whispered. I was whispering because I didn't want to scare the toad or any of the birds. Since then, I haven't picked up any wild animals, even snakes. The marsh is a beautiful place, and we should take care of it.

Mark the score that this paper should receive in the trait of SENTENCE FLUENCY. Read your rubric for Sentence Fluency to help you decide.

____ 1 ____ 2 ____ 3 ____ 4 ____ 5 ____ 6

Compare your score with your partner's. How did you do?

____ We matched exactly!

____ We matched within **one point**—pretty good!

____ We were **two points or more** apart. We need to discuss this.

Sample Paper 20: Drinking Fountains

Objectives

This paper was selected for its smooth, natural flow. Use it to show students how varied sentence beginnings and lengths make writing pleasant to read—aloud or silently.

Materials

Student Rubric for Sentence Fluency (Teacher's Guide page 77)

Sample Paper 20: Drinking Fountains (Teacher's Guide page 179 and/or Transparency 20)

Scoring the Paper

1. Give each student a copy of the sample paper and the Student Rubric for Sentence Fluency. Use the rubric to focus students' attention on the key features of the trait of SENTENCE FLUENCY. In particular, students should look and listen for differences in sentence beginnings and sentence lengths, run-ons, and a smooth, natural flow of words.

2. Have students think about this question as they listen to you read the paper: *How would you describe the sentence fluency?*

3. Ask students to score the paper *individually,* using the rubric. They should mark their scores in writing, putting an **X** in the appropriate blank. (If students do not have copies of the sample paper, they can write on separate sheets of paper.)

4. Ask students to compare their responses with those of a partner. They should take a few minutes to talk about the paper and ask each other questions.

© Great Source. Copying is prohibited.

Discussing the Paper

Discuss the paper with the class. Ask students to say what scores they gave the paper and why. The *why* is the most important part in deepening their understanding. Use the following questions to encourage discussion:

- Did many sentences in this paper begin differently? What effect did this have on fluency?

- Did this paper sound smooth when you heard it read aloud?

- Did you read the paper aloud yourself when discussing it with your partner? If you did, was it easy to read?

- Could this writer do anything to improve the fluency? If so, what?

*Rationale for the Score**

Most students should see this paper as **strong.** It received a **5** on the 6-point rubric because many sentences begin differently, it has no fluency flaws, and it is smooth, natural, and easy to read aloud or silently. Some readers may find "Drinking Fountains" as fluent as "The Marsh" but the sentence beginnings in "The Marsh" were a bit more varied. However, this paper is written well.

Extensions

1. If students have read and scored "The Marsh," ask them to compare that paper to this one in terms of fluency. Which do they find more fluent? "The Marsh" may be slightly more fluent, but there is no "right answer" to this.

2. Who invented the drinking fountain? Find out, and then ask each student to draft a short note to this person that he or she will find fluent and delightful to read. (The content of the note is up to the writer.) Imagine that the inventor might read this note aloud to a friend.

3. Suppose the inventor of the drinking fountain were given some sort of award for "Best Invention of the Year." Ask students to draft the short speech the inventor might give upon receiving this award. Remind them that members of the audience will hear the speech, but will not have copies to read to themselves. Emphasize the importance of fluency in both writing and speaking.

*See Teacher's Guide page 198 for a 5-point rubric and page 212 for the score.

name: .... date: ....

Sample Paper 20: Sentence Fluency

Drinking Fountains

Aren't drinking fountains a great idea? You can get a drink of water without having to use a glass! Just turn the knob or press the button and whoosh! Cold, fresh water comes flowing out. Just bend your head and drink.

Of course, it wasn't always this easy. Years ago, people walking on city streets had nowhere to go for a drink of water if they got thirsty. Then some observant citizen recognized an opportunity and invented the drinking fountain. At first, drinking fountains were built on the sidewalks so people could drink whenever they wanted to. But then someone decided that the fountain might attract bugs or that the water could get dirty. So, many drinking fountains were moved inside to keep them clean. Fortunately, things have changed. Today, we have fountains inside and outside, and we can use them anytime, anywhere.

Mark the score that this paper should receive in the trait of SENTENCE FLUENCY. Read your rubric for Sentence Fluency to help you decide.

____ 1 ____ 2 ____ 3 ____ 4 ____ 5 ____ 6

Compare your score with your partner's. How did you do?

____ We matched exactly!

____ We matched within **one point**—pretty good!

____ We were **two points or more** apart. We need to discuss this.

Unit 6
[Conventions]

Sample Paper 21: Braids

Objectives

This paper was selected because it contains enough errors to make reading it difficult. Use it to show students that conventional errors can slow a reader down and sometimes get in the way of the writer's message.

Materials

Student Rubric for Conventions (Teacher's Guide page 95)

Sample Paper 21: Braids (Teacher's Guide page 182 and/or Transparency 21)

Scoring the Paper

1. Give each student a copy of the sample paper and the Student Rubric for Conventions. Use the rubric to focus students' attention on the key features of the trait of CONVENTIONS. In particular, students should look for missing or repeated words and any errors in spelling, punctuation, grammar, and capitalization.

2. Have students think about these questions as they read the paper: *Are there many errors in this piece of writing? Do the errors affect your understanding of what the author is trying to say?*

3. Ask students to score the paper *individually*, using the rubric. They should mark their scores in writing, putting an **X** in the appropriate blank. (If students do not have copies of the sample paper, they can write on separate sheets of paper.)

4. Ask students to compare their responses with those of a partner. They should take a few minutes to talk about the paper and ask each other questions.

Discussing the Paper

Discuss the paper with the class. Ask students to say what scores they gave the paper and why. The *why* is the most important part in deepening their understanding. Use the following questions to encourage discussion:

- As you read through this paper, did you notice many errors? A few errors? Almost no errors?
- Do writing mistakes in this piece slow your reading? Where?
- Could the writer get this piece published? Why or why not?

*Rationale for the Score**

Most students should see this paper as weak. It received a **2** on the 6-point rubric because it contains many errors of various kinds. The errors could slow a reader down (especially a less experienced student reader), but they do not really distort meaning. At the same time, this piece would need a lot of work before it could be published.

Extensions

1. Have students work in pairs. Ask them to count the number of errors they find in the paper. Then, as a class, make a continuum and do a tally. Make a record of the type and number of errors each student pair finds. (Do not expect Grade 4 editors to find all errors, but anyone who comes close should get a round of applause.)

2. Have student partners work together to practice editing skills. Give each pair two to three lines from the paper to examine. Ask them to correct as many errors as they can. Then put up your overhead copy, and insert any corrections students have found. Add additional corrections yourself if they miss any errors.

3. Invite students to draft a short note to the writer, making any suggestions they think are appropriate for helping him or her improve performance in conventions.

*See Teacher's Guide page 199 for a 5-point rubric and page 212 for the score.

Sample Paper 21: Conventions

Braids

Do you want a cool new hair dew? If you do then hear are the derections right on this pies of papper.

First of all you need a come and two rubber bands Then part the hair into two diffrent groups. Divide the first group in three parts. Next take one of the end parts and put it over the middle do the same with the other end part and put it over the middle. Then keep going back and forth, puting each end over the middle. Keep on going until you gets to the bottom.

Then rap rubber band around the group of hair Do the same thing to the other group of hair. Then take some hair spray out and spray it on the brades. Then you will have a cool new hair dew.

Mark the score that this paper should receive in the trait of CONVENTIONS. Read your rubric for Conventions to help you decide.

___ 1 ___ 2 ___ 3 ___ 4 ___ 5 ___ 6

Compare your score with your partner's. How did you do?

___ We matched exactly!

___ We matched within **one point**—pretty good!

___ We were **two points or more** apart. We need to discuss this.

Sample Paper 22: How to Make a Skateboard

Objectives

This paper was selected because it contains enough errors to make reading difficult. Use it to show students that conventional errors, if serious enough, can get in the way of meaning.

Materials

Student Rubric for Conventions (Teacher's Guide page 95)

Sample Paper 22: How to Make a Skateboard (Teacher's Guide page 185 and/or Transparency 22)

Scoring the Paper

1. Give each student a copy of the sample paper and the Student Rubric for Conventions. Use the rubric to focus students' attention on the key features of the trait of CONVENTIONS. In particular, students should look for missing or repeated words and any errors in spelling, punctuation, grammar, and capitalization.

2. Have students think about this question as they read the paper: *Is this piece of writing ready to be published? Why or why not?*

3. Ask students to score the paper *individually,* using the rubric. They should mark their scores in writing, putting an **X** in the appropriate blank. (If students do not have copies of the sample paper, they can write on separate sheets of paper.)

4. Ask students to compare their responses with those of a partner. They should take a few minutes to talk about the paper and ask each other questions.

5. After three or four minutes, ask students to write the reasons for scoring the paper as they did.

Discussing the Paper

Discuss the paper with the class. Ask students to say what scores they gave the paper and why. The *why* is the most important part in deepening their understanding. Use the following questions to encourage discussion:

- As you read through this paper, did you notice many errors? A few errors? Almost no errors?

- Do the mistakes in this piece slow your reading? Do they ever get in the way of the writer's message? If so, where?

- How much work would it take to get this paper ready for publication? A lot? A little?

Rationale for the Score*

Most students should see this paper as **weak.** It received a **1** on the 6-point rubric because it contains many errors (editing this would be quite a task), and some errors—especially in the second half—make the message hard to decipher. The errors will definitely slow a careful reader. Missing words, the use of *But* for *Put,* missing punctuation, and other errors show that this writer is not in control of conventions.

Extensions

1. Ask students to count the number of errors in the passage. Do a general continuum in which students vote for one of the following: *many errors, some errors, a few small errors,* or *hardly any errors.*

2. Do not expect fourth graders to correct (or watch someone else correct) the errors in this piece during a single class session. Break the task into manageable portions by looking at one or two sentences at a time for editing practice.

*See Teacher's Guide page 199 for a 5-point rubric and page 213 for the score.

Sample Paper 22: Conventions

How to Make a Skateboard

Today i am going to tell you how to a skateboard. Thats what I do every day after school. So heres how you first need a Big block of wood. Then you cut the block of wood in a skateboard shape? But 8 holes. 4 on the middle right. 4 on the middle left. The holes are for the screws that go in the trucks and yours the bolts and put in on the botom side of the screws and titan them. You need wheels to put on the trucks on the side the board. Paint the skateboard your choice and But the grip tap on the top of the skateboard (the grip tap helps you hold on to the board) and their you have it a home made skateboard be sure to ware you helmet when you ride it

Mark the score that this paper should receive in the trait of CONVENTIONS. Read your rubric for Conventions to help you decide. Then write the reasons for your score.

_____ 1 _____ 2 _____ 3 _____ 4 _____ 5 _____ 6

_____

_____

_____

Compare your score with your partner's. How did you do?

_____ We matched exactly!

_____ We matched within **one point**—pretty good!

_____ We were **two points or more** apart. We need to discuss this.

Sample Paper 23: Bike Safety

Objectives

This paper was selected because it contains few, if any, errors. This writer has a firm grasp of conventions, so you can use the paper to show that strong conventions help keep the message clear and make the paper easy to read.

Materials

Student Rubric for Conventions (Teacher's Guide page 95)

Sample Paper 23: Bike Safety (Teacher's Guide page 188 and/or Transparency 23)

Scoring the Paper

1. Give each student a copy of the sample paper and the Student Rubric for Conventions. Use the rubric to focus students' attention on the key features of the trait of CONVENTIONS. In particular, students should look and listen for missing or repeated words and any errors in spelling, punctuation, grammar, and capitalization.

2. Have students think about this question as they read the paper: *Is this piece of writing ready to be published? Why or why not?*

3. Ask students to score the paper *individually,* using the rubric. They should mark their scores in writing, putting an **X** in the appropriate blank. (If students do not have copies of the sample paper, they can write on separate sheets of paper.)

4. Ask students to compare their responses with those of a partner. They should take a few minutes to talk about the paper and ask each other questions.

5. After three or four minutes, ask students to write the reasons for scoring the paper as they did.

Discussing the Paper

Discuss the paper with the class. Ask students to say what scores they gave the paper and why. The *why* is the most important part in deepening their understanding. Use the following questions to encourage discussion:

- As you read through this paper, did you notice many errors? A few errors? Almost no errors?
- Is there any place in this paper where conventional errors slow your reading?
- Do you think this paper is ready for publication? Why or why not?
- Do this writer's conventions make the paper easy to read?

Rationale for the Score*

Most students should see this paper as **strong.** It received a **6** on the 6-point rubric because it contains virtually no errors. It could be argued that the three points the writer makes should be in separate paragraphs. Certainly the paper could be set up that way, but because the points are so short, they could also be presented together. Overall, this writer is very much in control of punctuation, spelling, grammar, and capitalization. The absence of errors makes the paper easy to read.

Extensions

1. Suppose this writer were to write a short article called "The Secret to Good Conventions." What secret might the writer share? Ask each student to write a short article that could appear in a school newsletter. Each article should be at least five sentences long and should suggest at least one way to use conventions well.

2. Perhaps this writer will apply for a job as an editor. Draft a letter of application the writer might send to a future employer, explaining the writer's skills in working with conventions. The letter should be at least 5 or 6 sentences long and contain some detail about what this writer/editor can do.

3. Have students write a conventions quiz. Tell each of them to write a sentence containing just ONE conventional error. Then ask them to exchange sentences with a partner to see whether they can find each other's errors. When students are finished, compare results. Who had the toughest, trickiest error to correct? Would any of the editing quizzes have stumped the writer of "Bike Safety"?

*See Teacher's Guide page 199 for a 5-point rubric and page 213 for the score.

Sample Paper 23: Conventions

Bike Safety

There are three important things to remember if you want to be safe when you ride your bike. The most important thing is to wear a helmet. Lots of people do not like helmets. I don't! They make your hair look really funny! If you fall, though, you will be glad you have that helmet. The second thing is not to ride where there is a lot of traffic. Many drivers never even see bikers. They are too busy talking on their cell phones or listening to the radio. That is why many bikers get hit by cars. The third thing is to obey all traffic signs. You might think a red light, for example, is just for cars. No way! It is for you, too, if you are on a bike. You should also signal when you make a right or left turn. So those are some ways to be safe when you ride. Goodbye, and have fun on your bike!

Mark the score that this paper should receive in the trait of CONVENTIONS. Read your rubric for Conventions to help you decide. Then write the reasons for your score.

_____ 1 _____ 2 _____ 3 _____ 4 _____ 5 _____ 6

_____

_____

Compare your score with your partner's. How did you do?

_____ We matched exactly!

_____ We matched within **one point**—pretty good!

_____ We were **two points or more** apart. We need to discuss this.

Sample Paper 24: Night of Terror

Objectives

This paper was selected because it contains some errors—yet more things are done correctly than incorrectly. Use this paper to show that conventional errors can be distracting, even when they do not get in the way of meaning.

Materials

Student Rubric for Conventions (Teacher's Guide page 95)

Sample Paper 24: Night of Terror (Teacher's Guide page 191 and/or Transparency 24)

Scoring the Paper

1. Give each student a copy of the sample paper and the Student Rubric for Conventions. Use the rubric to focus students' attention on the key features of the trait of CONVENTIONS. In particular, students should look for missing or repeated words and any errors in spelling, punctuation, grammar, and capitalization.

2. Have students think about this question as they read the paper: *Has this writer done a careful job of editing? How do you know?*

3. Ask students to score the paper *individually,* using the rubric. They should mark their scores in writing, putting an **X** in the appropriate blank. (If students do not have copies of the sample paper, they can write on separate sheets of paper.)

4. Ask students to compare their responses with those of a partner. They should take a few minutes to talk about the paper and ask each other questions.

Discussing the Paper

Discuss the paper with the class. Ask students to say what scores they gave the paper and why. The *why* is the most important part in deepening their understanding. Use the following questions to encourage discussion:

- As you read through this paper, did you notice many errors? A few errors? Almost no errors?

- Do conventional errors in this paper slow your reading? If so, where are these places?

- Do you think this paper is ready for publication? Why or why not?

- Does this writer do many things correctly? Name one or two.

*Rationale for the Score**

Most students should see this paper as somewhat **strong.** It received a **4** on the 6-point rubric because it has more strengths than problems—yet there are quite a few errors. It needs a good editorial review before it's ready for publication. Sample errors include *wake* for *woke, to* for *too,* lowercase *i,* no apostrophe in *didnt, smeled* for *smelled,* shift in tense (turned on the flashlight and our whole deck *lights* up), *expect* for *expected, diner* for *dinner,* and no punctuation following *What a relief.* On the other hand, the writer spells many words correctly, uses proper grammar most of the time, and uses punctuation and capital letters correctly in most cases. Though not ready for publication, the piece shows a writer with growing control over conventions.

Extensions

1. Have students identify this writer's MAIN problem with conventions. Then have partners work together to create a dialogue between **The Problem** and **The Writer.** The Problem is out to stump The Writer whenever possible. The Problem will turn up in a paper every time it has a chance. The Writer, of course, is hoping to stamp out The Problem! Ask students to create a conversation the two of them (The Problem and The Writer) might have, using correct conventions.

2. Have students edit "Night of Terror" for conventions. Because it contains few errors, it is a good piece on which to practice. Be sure to compare students' edited drafts, and review errors one by one. Students who find and correct ten errors or more could go on the "Eagle Eye" list for the week.

*See Teacher's Guide page 199 for a 5-point rubric and page 213 for the score.

Sample Paper 24: Conventions

Night of Terror

One night my mom wake up and whispered to my dad, "I hear something!" I heard it to, and I also heard my mom, so i got up to see what the problem was. Mom grabed the flashlight she keeps under her bed and we went downstairs where the noise was coming from. I was really scared, but I did not want Mom to know that so I was trying not to breathe too loud or anything. She crept over to the window and the noise got louder. I didnt want to go at first, but then I get curious so I went over to the window too. "Ready?" Mom asked me and I was shivering so hard I didnt feel like talking so I just nodded yes. She turned on the flashlight and our whole deck lights up! I expect to see a burglar out there because I could still here the noise, but instead we saw a big old raccoon! He was trying very hard to come in our back door. I think he smeled the hamburgers we cooked for diner. "What a relief" Mom said.

Mark the score that this paper should receive in the trait of CONVENTIONS. Read your rubric for Conventions to help you decide.

___ 1 ___ 2 ___ 3 ___ 4 ___ 5 ___ 6

Compare your score with your partner's. How did you do?

____ We matched exactly!

____ We matched within **one point**—pretty good!

____ We were **two points or more** apart. We need to discuss this.

Appendix:

Using a 5-Point Rubric

For your convenience, we have included in this appendix a 5-point student and teacher rubric for each trait and a score for each Sample Paper based on the 5-point rubric. Although we have always recommended the 6-point rubric, the 5-point rubric has certain advantages.

The 5-point rubric is simple to use and to internalize. Performance is defined at only three levels: **weak** (point 1), **somewhat strong** (point 3), and **strong** or proficient (point 5). The 4 and the 2 on the 5-point scale are compromise scores. Therefore, if a performance is slightly stronger than a 3, but not quite strong enough to warrant a 5, it would receive a 4. Because raters think in terms of "weak, somewhat strong, and strong" in assigning scores, this is a simple system to follow.

Performance in writing is defined at only three levels, so it is possible to make those written definitions longer and more detailed than when defining *every* level. Many users like this richer text, especially if they are learning traits for the first time or if they are looking for language to use in teaching traits to students.

Few differences exist conceptually between these rubrics. Remember that the key reason to use rubrics with students is to teach the concepts: *ideas, organization, voice, word choice, sentence fluency,* and *conventions.* We want students to understand what we mean, for example, by good *organization,* and one way of doing this is to have them score writing samples. The particular rubric used is less important than whether a student sees a paper as weak, strong, or somewhere between those two points. We want students to distinguish between writing that works and writing that needs revision; whether they define a strong performance as a 5 or 6 is much less important than their understanding of why a paper is strong or weak. The numbers are merely a kind of shorthand that allows students and teachers to discuss competency in simple terms.

Keep in mind, too, that all rubrics are essentially 3-point rubrics: weak, somewhat strong, and strong. On the 5-point rubric, these performance levels correspond to the scores of 1, 3 and 5 respectively. On the 6-point rubric, each level is divided into two parts, high and low. Thus, a score of 1 represents the lowest weak score, a score of 2 is a somewhat higher weak score, and so on. Scores of 3 and 4 represent the two levels of the somewhat strong category, 5 and 6 the two levels of strength. On the 6-point rubric, *all* performance levels are defined.

We hope that these distinctions help clarify the very slight differences between these rubrics. Use the rubrics with which you are most familiar or with which you feel most comfortable. Regardless of your choice, you will be teaching your students about the basic, underlying components that define good writing—and that is what counts!

Ideas

5 **My paper has details that make my main idea clear.**

- Readers can tell that I know a lot about this topic.

- It's easy to determine my main idea.

- I chose my details carefully. They are important and interesting.

- I left out the "filler."

3 **My paper is clear in some parts, but I need more information. My details are too general.**

- I know some things about this topic. I wish I knew more.

- Readers can identify my main idea.

- Some of my "details" are things most people already know.

- Some information is not needed. It's just filler.

- This topic feels big—maybe I'm trying to tell too much.

1 **I'm still working on what I want to say.**

- Help! I don't know enough about this topic to write about it.

- Can readers identify my main idea? I'm not sure myself!

- I need better details. I just tossed in anything I could think of.

- I was writing to fill space.

Organization

5 **My paper is logical and easy to follow.**

- My lead gets the reader's attention and goes with the paper.

- Every detail seems to be in the right order.

- My paper follows a pattern that makes sense for this topic.

- It's easy to see how things are connected to my main point.

- My conclusion is just right! Readers will say, "Wow!"

3 **Readers can follow this paper most of the time.**

- My lead needs to be livelier—but at least it's there!

- Most details are in the right order.

- My paper follows a pattern most of the time.

- Most ideas are connected to my main point. Some aren't, though.

- My conclusion is OK. It's not exciting, but I have one.

1 **This paper is hard to follow.**

- My paper does not have a lead. I just started writing.

- I wrote ideas as they came into my head. I am not sure the order of details works.

- I don't see any real pattern here.

- I am not sure what my main point is, so it's hard to tell if my ideas are connected to it.

- I don't really have a conclusion. My paper just stops.

Voice

5 **This paper shows who I am. The reader can tell it's ME!**

- The reader will definitely want to share this aloud with someone.

- I love this topic, so lots of energy comes through.

- I'm writing for my readers, and I want them to love this topic as much as I do.

- This is just the right voice for this topic.

3 **Occasionally this paper shows who I am. The reader can hear ME sometimes. My voice comes and goes.**

- The reader may want to share parts of this paper aloud.

- This was an OK topic, but I couldn't get excited about it.

- I write for my readers some of the time. Other times, I don't think about them at all.

- I think this voice is OK for this topic.

1 **I don't hear much voice in this writing.**

- The reader probably will not want to share this paper aloud.

- This topic bored me, and I sound bored.

- I just wanted this to be over. I do not care much whether anyone reads it.

- My voice does not fit my topic well. It should be stronger or different.

Word Choice

5 **Every word helps make my writing clear and interesting.**

- My verbs have power. They energize my writing.

- My words paint a picture. The reader can tell just what I'm trying to say.

- I got rid of clutter (unnecessary words).

- I used some words that help the reader see, hear, touch, taste, or smell.

3 **My words are usually clear, but sometimes the reader may really need to concentrate.**

- A *few* of my verbs have power. Some could use more muscle.

- The reader can picture what I am talking about if he or she works at it a little.

- I got rid of some clutter, but I missed some, too.

- I thought about helping the reader see, hear, touch, taste, and smell, but sometimes I had trouble doing it.

1 **My words are hard to understand. I am not always sure what I'm trying to say.**

- I am not sure what verbs are. I probably don't have many in my paper.

- It's hard to picture what I am talking about. The writing is out of focus.

- Clutter? I think I might have some. I repeated words and used some words I did not need.

- I did not worry about helping the reader see, hear, touch, taste, or smell. I just used the first words I thought of.

Sentence Fluency

5 My writing is smooth. It sounds natural and is easy to read aloud.

- The reader will love reading this aloud. It is expressive.

- Almost all my sentences begin in different ways. Some are long, and some are short.

- If I used any dialogue, it sounds like real people talking.

3 Most of my writing is smooth. I might have some choppy sentences or run-ons, though.

- The reader won't stumble reading my paragraph aloud, but it might be hard to read my writing with expression.

- Many of my sentences begin the same way. Their length doesn't vary enough.

- If I used dialogue, it needs some work. Sometimes the people sound real, and sometimes they don't.

1 This is hard to read, even for me! The reader can't tell one sentence from another.

- The reader would have to work hard to read this aloud. I wouldn't want to read it aloud.

- All my sentences are the same. There is no variety at all.

- I tried, but my dialogue doesn't sound like real conversation.

Conventions

5 **A reader would have a hard time finding errors in this paper. It's ready to publish. I should know—I edited it myself.**

- I used conventions correctly to help make the meaning clear.

- I checked the spelling, punctuation, grammar, and capitalization. They are all correct.

- I read it silently to myself and aloud, too. I corrected every mistake I saw or heard.

3 **The reader will probably notice some errors. I need to go over this again and look carefully for errors!**

- I did a lot of things right, but I also made some errors. The reader might slow down once or twice because of the errors.

- I checked my spelling, punctuation, grammar, and capitalization. I think they are pretty good. I may have missed a few things, though.

- I did read it quickly. I guess I should read it again. I might hear mistakes that my eye missed.

1 **I made so many mistakes that a reader would have a hard time reading this.**

- This paper is so full of errors that it's hard to spot the things I did right.

- I forgot to check a lot of my spelling, punctuation, grammar, and capitalization. I did not really edit this at all.

- I did not read this over to myself. I guess I should. It needs work.

Ideas

5 **The paper has a clear, well-focused main idea and interesting, carefully chosen details that go beyond the obvious to support or expand that main idea.**

- The writer seems to know the topic well, and uses his or her knowledge to advantage.

- The main idea is easy to identify and understand. The paper is clearly focused.

- Thoughtfully selected details enhance the main idea and enlighten the reader.

- Filler—unneeded information—has been omitted. Every detail counts.

3 **The paper is clear, but the main idea is not well developed. There are few interesting or relevant details and more information is needed.**

- The writer seems to have a general grasp of the topic.

- The main idea is somewhat clear, or it can be inferred.

- Generalities abound, but little-known, significant, or intriguing details are rare.

- Some information is completely unnecessary.

1 **The writer does not have a clear topic or may need to narrow a topic that is still too broad to handle effectively.**

- The writer displays limited knowledge of the topic.

- The main idea is unclear, and the paper lacks focus.

- Details do not support or expand any larger message.

- Much of the writing simply fills space.

Organization

5 This writing is logical and easy to follow.

- The lead grabs the reader's attention and sets the tone for the paper.

- Every detail is in the right place.

- The paper follows an identifiable pattern (chronological order, comparison-contrast, or the like) that suits the topic.

- The reader can easily make connections between details and the writer's main ideas.

- The conclusion is complete. It is neither abrupt nor long-winded.

3 The reader can follow the direction of the paper most of the time.

- The paper has a lead, but it does not grab the reader's attention.

- Most details are in the right places.

- A pattern may not be immediately recognizable.

- It is possible to make connections between details and the writer's main idea. Some ideas are irrelevant.

- The paper has a conclusion though not a particularly strong one.

1 This paper is hard to follow.

- There is no lead. The writer just begins the paper.

- Few details are offered.

- It is difficult to identify any pattern within the writing.

- It is difficult to connect details to any main idea or story line; it may be hard to tell what the main point is.

- There is no conclusion. The paper just stops.

Voice

---

5 The writing is highly individual. It bears the definite imprint of this writer.

- The reader will want to share this aloud.

- The writer seems engaged by the topic, and a strong sense of personal energy comes through.

- This writer is writing for a particular audience.

- The voice is appropriate for the audience and topic.

---

3 The reader can hear the writer within the piece now and again. The voice comes and goes.

- The reader might share *moments* aloud, even if he or she does not share the whole piece.

- The writer seems comfortable with the topic but less than enthusiastic. Bursts of energy mix with lulls.

- This writer *could* be writing for a particular audience—or just to get the job done.

- The voice is acceptable for the topic and audience.

---

1 It would be difficult to identify this writer. There seems to be no voice in the writing.

- This piece is not yet ready to be shared aloud.

- The writer sounds bored; perhaps this topic did not work for him or her. It is hard to sense *any* personal engagement.

- The writer is not reaching out to any particular audience.

- This piece lacks voice, or the voice is not suited to the topic. It needs to be stronger or different in tone.

Word Choice

5 Every word helps make the writing clear and interesting.

- Strong verbs energize the writing.

- The words paint a vivid picture in the reader's mind. There are many noteworthy words and phrases.

- This writing is free of clutter.

- Sensory words (as appropriate) help readers see, hear, touch, taste, or smell images.

3 Most words and phrases are clear. Good writing is mixed with vague or misused language.

- A *few* strong verbs give life to the writing; more are necessary.

- The reader can often picture what the writer is talking about. Some language is either vague or overused.

- Some clutter may make the text wordy in spots.

- The writer misses opportunities to use sensory language.

1 Word choices are ineffective; they do not help convey the message.

- The writer does not use strong verbs. The language is flat.

- It's hard to picture what the writer is talking about. Vague or overused language gets in the way.

- The writing may be skimpy, or it may be buried in clutter.

- The writer does not make effective use of sensory language.

Sentence Fluency

5 **The writing sounds smooth and natural. It is easy to read aloud.**

- This paper can be read aloud with expression.

- Almost all of the sentences begin in different ways. Some are long, and some are short.

- If dialogue is used, it sounds like real conversation.

3 **The writing in this paper is smooth but has a few rough spots. Well-crafted sentences are interspersed with choppy wording or with run-ons.**

- Parts of this paper might be difficult to read aloud smoothly.

- Too many sentences begin the same way, and many sentences are the same length.

- Dialogue, if used, needs some work. Sometimes the language sounds real, and sometimes it sounds unnatural.

1 **This paper is hard to read aloud. Sometimes it is hard to tell where one sentence ends and the next one begins.**

- The reader will need to rehearse to read this paper aloud. Some verbal editing will be necessary, too.

- Variety in sentence lengths and beginnings is minimal.

- If dialogue is used, it sounds unnatural.

Conventions

5 **The writer is in control of conventions, and this paper is ready to publish.**

- The writer has used conventions correctly, which helps clarify meaning.

- The spelling, capitalization, punctuation, and grammar are, for the most part, correct.

- The writer has read the paper both silently and aloud and has corrected every (or nearly every) mistake.

3 **The writer is somewhat in control of conventions. A careful proofreading will prepare this text for publication.**

- Correct use of conventions enhance meaning in parts of the text. A few errors may catch a reader's eye or slow the reading. Errors do not distort meaning.

- Spelling, capitalization, punctuation, and grammar errors are at an acceptable level and could easily be corrected.

- The writer has read the paper through at least once, but a second reading—silent or oral—could help identify additional errors.

1 **This writer is not yet in control of conventions. Many errors need correcting before this text is ready to publish.**

- Numerous errors slow the reader and occasionally get in the way of the writer's message.

- The text contains many errors in spelling, capitalization, punctuation, and grammar.

- The writer does not appear to have read this paper either silently or aloud. The paper should be edited by the writer and perhaps by an editing partner.

Rationales for the Scores Using the 5-point Rubric

Unit 1: Ideas

Sample Paper 1: *The Light Bulb*

Rationale for the Score

Most students should see this paper as fairly **weak.** We have given it a score of **2** on the 5-point rubric, although some students may see it as a 3. It has a main idea: Light bulbs are useful. However this idea is far too general and has little support. Many of the items mentioned in the paper—we wouldn't have video games, TVs, or computers—have nothing to do with light bulbs. These comments relate more to the issue of electricity (and in fact, this is probably the writer's underlying topic). The writer assumes that without light bulbs, we would not have electricity, so we would need candles and torches; this notion shows inexact knowledge of the subject. On the positive side, the paper is fairly clear and easy to understand. However, it never addresses the main issue: what makes *light bulbs* so useful.

Sample Paper 2: *Cookies!*

Rationale for the Score

Most students should see this paper as **strong.** We have given it a score of **4** on the 5-point rubric, and it only misses receiving a 5 because most of the information, though useful and interestingly presented, is known to most readers. Some students may wish to give this paper a 5. This writer is writing from experience, and she knows her topic very well: buying cookie dough to save time, preheating the oven, recognizing what the dough feels like, using oven mitts to avoid burns, and so on. Of course, if you do not wish to read about cookies, the paper may seem less than exciting. But this is not a good reason for lowering the score. The question is whether the writer has presented *this topic* clearly and thoroughly.

Sample Paper 3: *A Hard Thing to Do*

Rationale for the Score

Most students should see this paper as **strong.** We have given it a score of **5** on the 5-point rubric because the main idea—that making a bed is difficult and frustrating—is exceptionally clear and well supported by unusual details that come from the writer's own experience. This writer shares a clear method for how to make a bed. Anyone who has struggled making a bed shoved against a wall can appreciate this writer's frustration as well as the innovative solutions to the problem.

Sample Paper 4: *Something I Am Good At*

Rationale for the Score

Most students should see this paper as **weak.** We have given it a score of **2** on the 5-point rubric because it lacks focus and does not develop any one idea. Details are sketchy and limited; the lead is a list of things the writer does well. The paper also contains filler—especially the references to the sister playing the piano and the writer playing baseball next year. The main idea seems to be "I am good at basketball because I practice," but the paper contains too much unrelated information.

Unit 2: Organization

Sample Paper 5: *Lunchtime*

Rationale for the Score

Most students should see this paper as **strong.** We have given it a score of **5** on the 5-point rubric because it is easy to follow and includes every step at the right time. The lead is fresh and lively—*I think I'll fix myself a turkey sandwich . . . Sophie style.* The ending works well, too.

Sample Paper 6: *How to Walk Your Rat*

Rationale for the Score

Most students should see this paper as **strong.** We have given it a score of **4** on the 5-point rubric because it is easy to follow and has a strong lead. The conclusion also works, but some revision could make it more original. Also, the writer could have put in one or two more details about how to get the harness on the rat. This part starts out well, but the writer has omitted some of the necessary steps. Other details, however, are well organized.

Sample Paper 7: *Not Your Normal Wednesday*

Rationale for the Score

Most students should see this paper as **weak.** We have given it a score of **2** on the 5-point rubric because it meanders randomly from topic to topic with little concern for giving the reader any sense of direction. The lead is engaging (almost enough to push the paper to a 3), but we get no real explanation of how this Wednesday is unusual. Instead, the writer leapfrogs from bubbles to a crazy bus ride, then to a photo shoot, and then to animal habitats. A strong central idea clearly stated at the beginning could help keep things more orderly. Right now, it's hard to see how one thing goes with another. The conclusion also needs work.

Sample Paper 8: *Schools*

Rationale for the Score

Most students should see this paper as **weak.** We have given it a score of **1** on the 5-point rubric because it wanders randomly and does not connect key points to any main idea. The topic wanders from why schools are important to a general discussion of schools. The lead is weak, and the conclusion is nonexistent; the paper suddenly stops with the comment on how kids get to school. Transitions are missing or weak. There is no identifiable pattern to the organization.

Unit 3: Voice

Sample Paper 9: *The Underground City*

Rationale for the Score

Most students should see this paper as **weak.** We have given it a score of **2** on the 5-point rubric because it has very little energy. The writer sounds bored and provides only facts. It is hard to tell *how* this writer feels through most of the paper. Also, it's hard to *hear* the voice when the paper is read aloud.

Sample Paper 10: *Swimming*

Rationale for the Score

Most students should see this paper as *somewhat* **strong,** but not consistently so. We have given it a score of **3** on the 5-point rubric because it is not consistently strong in voice. It is easy to hear how proud this writer is about overcoming her fear of water. The sentences "I was doing it. I was swimming!" convey the strongest moment in the paper.

Sample Paper 11: *Drawing Teddy Roosevelt*

Rationale for the Score

Most students should see this paper as **strong.** This paper received the top score of **5** on the 5-point rubric. The writer uses a clear, strong voice. The writer also uses detail and humor to put voice into a piece that could have been very matter-of-fact. The writer never sounds bored, though the humor is on the dry side. (Don't be surprised if some scores fall below the 5 level.) Much of the voice comes from the writer's struggles and unflinching honesty about his or her inability to draw well. Poor Teddy's teeth! Who could forget?

Sample Paper 12: *Our New Dog*

Rationale for the Score

Most students should see this paper as **weak.** It is tempting to give it a higher score because of the topic. However, it is not the topic that creates voice; it is how the writer approaches that topic. The lack of energy and detail explain why the piece received a score of **1** on the 5-point rubric. The dog does not even have a name. We know the mom did not want the dog at first, but later she lets it stay. Why? The reader has no idea, nor can the reader hear any of the characters speak. There is no dialogue. The children forget to feed the dog, and this is easy to believe because they do not sound excited about this new pet.

Unit 4: Word Choice

Sample Paper 13: *Our Field Trip to Wood World*

Rationale for the Score

Most students should see this paper as **weak.** The words *cool, a lot,* and *super* appear too often, and because they are imprecise, we do not get a clear picture of the events that happened on the field trip. The paper lacks strong verbs and sensory language to paint a picture in the reader's mind. Consequently, we give it a **2** on the 5-point rubric. Some students may even see it as a 1, though we think it's somewhat stronger than that since the general message does come through.

Sample Paper 14: *How a Quarterback Throws a Football*

Rationale for the Score

Most students should see this paper as **strong.** We gave it a **5** on the 5-point rubric. Some students may wish to drop it to a 4 because the first few sentences are not as strong as the rest; there is a lot of "lining up on the line!" Still, the first few sentences are clear, and words are used with precision. The writer makes extensive use of verbs, especially in the second part of the paper: *drops back, seeks, rotates, gets sacked, steps* *forward, follows through, score, scream,* and *celebrate.* The writing is clean and concise, free of extraneous words. It is easy to picture what is happening, even if you know little about football.

Sample Paper 15: *Why Spiders Have Eight Eyes*

Rationale for the Score

Most students should see this paper as **strong.** We gave it a **5** on the 5-point rubric. It has exceptionally strong verbs, precise language throughout, and many good sensory details: the animals feel *exhausted,* Spider feels *selfish,* Spider *crunches* as he devours Mouse. The phrasing is explicit: *flew into a rage,* for example. Modifiers are used well, too: *gruesome, exhausted,* and *selfish* are clear and exact. Students should have little trouble finding favorite words and phrases.

Sample Paper 16: *Our Old House*

Rationale for the Score

Most students should see this paper as fairly **weak.** We gave it a **2** on the 5-point rubric. It is clear in a general sense, but it lacks flair. The verbs are weak, and many words are vague or overused: *neat, cool, really,* and so on. The language needs an energy boost!

Unit 5: Sentence Fluency

Sample Paper 17: *A Cool Trip*

Rationale for the Score

Most students should see this paper as fairly **weak.** We gave it a **2** on the 5-point rubric because it has repetitive sentence beginnings and several run-on sentences. It is awkward to read aloud. Eliminating the run-ons and varying the sentence beginnings would make the writing smoother and easier to read.

Sample Paper 18: *Dear Mom*

Rationale for the Score

Most students should see this paper as fairly **weak.** It received a **2** on the 5-point rubric because the writer repeatedly uses *It, I,* or *You* as sentence openers. In addition, the overall piece is quite choppy because sentences tend to be short and of similar length. Sentence combining would help.

Sample Paper 19: *The Marsh*

Rationale for the Score

Most students should see this paper as very **strong.** We gave it a **5** on the 5-point rubric because virtually every sentence begins differently, because there are no fluency problems, and because the sound is smooth. It's a pleasure to read aloud. In addition, the dialogue sounds authentic. This piece has a natural sound that makes it a good model for fluency.

Sample Paper 20: *Drinking Fountains*

Rationale for the Score

Most students should see this paper as **strong.** We gave it a **4** on the 5-point rubric because many sentences begin differently, because it has no fluency flaws, and because overall, it is smooth, natural, and easy to read aloud or silently. Some readers may find "Drinking Fountains" as fluent as "The Marsh," but the sentence beginnings in "The Marsh" are a bit more varied. However, this paper is well written.

Unit 6: Conventions

Sample Paper 21: *Braids*

Rationale for the Score

Most students should see this paper as quite **weak.** We gave it a **2** on the 5-point rubric because it contains many errors of various kinds. The errors may slow the reader (especially a less experienced student reader), but they do not really distort meaning. At the same time, this piece would need a thorough revision before it could be published.

Sample Paper 22: *How to Make a Skateboard*

Rationale for the Score

Most students should see this paper as very **weak.** We gave it a **1** on the 5-point rubric because it contains many errors (editing this would be quite a task), and some errors—especially in the second half—make the message hard to decipher. The errors will definitely slow a careful reader. Missing words, the use of *But* for *Put,* missing punctuation, and other errors show that this writer is not in control of conventions.

Sample Paper 23: *Bike Safety*

Rationale for the Score

Most students should see this paper as very **strong.** We gave it a **5** on the 5-point rubric because it contains virtually no errors. It could be argued that the three points the writer makes should be in separate paragraphs. Certainly the paper could be set up that way, but since the points are so short, they could also be presented together. Overall, this writer is very much in control of punctuation, spelling, grammar, and capitalization. The absence of errors makes the paper easy to read.

Sample Paper 24: *Night of Terror*

Rationale for the Score

Most students should see this paper as somewhat **strong.** The choice between scores of 3 and 4 is a tough call. We gave it a **3** on the 5-point rubric because it has more strengths than problems—yet there are quite a few errors. It needs a good editorial review before it's ready for publication. Sample errors include *wake* for *woke, to* for *too,* lowercase *i,* no apostrophe in *didnt, smeled* for *smelled,* shift in tense (turned on the flashlight and our whole deck *lights* up), *expect* for *expected, diner* for *dinner,* and no punctuation following *What a relief.* On the other hand, the writer spells many words correctly, uses proper grammar most of the time, and uses punctuation and capital letters correctly in most cases. Though not ready for publication, the piece shows a writer with growing control over conventions.